The anatomy of the rise and fall
of the 21st Government

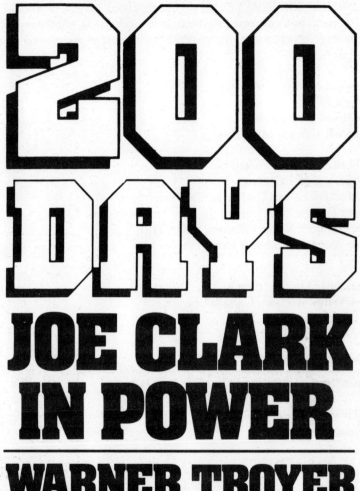

200 DAYS

JOE CLARK IN POWER

WARNER TROYER
PREFACE BY DALTON CAMP

Personal Library, Publishers
Toronto

Personal Library, Publishers
Suite 439
17 Queen Street East
Toronto, Canada M5C 1P9

Publisher: Glenn Edward Witmer
Editor: Jennifer Glossop
Production Editor: Catherine Van Baren
Cover Design: First Image
Composition: Rupert Bisram/Video Text
Page Assembly: Robert Kemp/Video Text

**Distributed to the trade by
John Wiley and Sons Canada Ltd.
22 Worcester Road
Rexdale, Ontario M9W 1L1**

Canadian Cataloguing in Publication Data

Troyer, Warner, 1932-
200 days

ISBN 0-920510-05-1

1. Canada - Politics and government - 1968-   *
2. Clark, Joe, 1939-   I. Title.

FC630.T76   971.064'5   C80-094102-0
F1034.2.T76

Printed and bound in Canada by The Hunter Rose Company Ltd.

Contents

Preface by Dalton Camp   7

Introduction   18

Chapter One   22
Jasper: The Seeds of Destruction

Chapter Two   38
Joe Clark: A Profile

Chapter Three   46
The Spearbearers: Murray and McTeer

Chapter Four   54
The Embassy Move: A Metaphor of Method

Interregnum   74

Chapter Five   76
Ottawa: Life in the Hothouse

Chapter Six   108
Foreign Affairs: Playing in the Major Leagues

Chapter Seven   131
The Provinces: The Community of Communities

Chapter Eight   154
Clark's Parliament: Government in Free Fall

Chapter Nine   175
Clark and the Voters: Victory by Default

Chapter Ten   186
The Coroner's Verdict

"It is our politicians who fashion
the compromises which keep all sorts
of men and women in the widely
dispersed and varied regions of
our country moving forward together.
And the only certainty they face —
from the moment of their election —
is that sooner or later they are
going to be defeated and thereafter
largely ignored."
— Michael Pitfield,
November, 1979.

Preface
by Dalton Camp

A bank manager I knew in London while I was a student at the London School of Economics once asked me what course of studies I was pursuing. I told him I was studying political science.

"Ah," he said, disdainfully, "the meanest of the sciences."

And so it is. Political scientists, I have observed, exhaust themselves in trying to find out why things happen and, once they think they know, in further attempting to organize their findings into some coherent system.

But so perverse is politics — not to mention the politicians — that systems and theories collapse under the weight of exceptions. While there is much established order in physics and chemistry, there is mostly chaos in politics, so that the very term "political science" may be a misnomer. After all, our most adroit, adept, and successful practitioner of politics, Mackenzie King, was also a close student of the supernatural: he must have been on to something.

Still, human curiosity fuels the need to know, a need

immediately served by journalists and, later on, by historians. For those impatient to know what happened to the Progressive Conservative minority government that came to power in Canada after the election of May 22, 1979, and was abruptly defeated in Parliament seven months later, we can only rely on the quick reflexes and resources of journalists. We will have to wait longer for the historians.

Warner Troyer sets out here to put down in an orderly manner the events that led us to the altogether unlikely federal election in the winter of 1980. It is an enterprise worthy of the considerable effort involved because so much seems to have happened in so short a time. Moreover, so much of it was so contrary to common sense expectations that even a decent chronology would be helpful. Troyer has given us more than that, helped, no doubt, by the hard-nose of the professional journalist behind which there lies a wealth of knowledge of politics, and of politicians. And, along with that, a discerning talent for sifting wheat from chaff.

Political prophecy — by which I mean a leap in surmise in advance of relevant data — is a mug's game. Hindsight is not only easier, but safer. Even so, it was possible to foresee trouble for the Tories even before the government fell. "The Conservatives could be in desperate trouble by next fall," wrote Geoffrey Stevens, in an early December column in *The Globe and Mail*. But not even Stevens could predict the desperate straits they would be in before Christmas, 1979.

The Tories were in some trouble even before they were elected in May. The televised debate between the party leaders hurt the Conservatives more than they realized, or would admit; after that, they nervously sat on their lead, even while it was melting.

Not only did the Tories sit on their lead, they sat on their victory. After the election one got the impression that the winners had settled into Jasper, Alberta, for a celebration of indeterminate length. Anyway, it took them four months to get over the celebration and three more to find themselves out on the hustings again.

In the meantime, I suspect, they perfected the mythology of their triumphant passage from opposition to government, the deadliest myth being that the Liberals had not been defeated, but that the Tories had been elected. Having seen more than one Liberal government interred, I know how appealing it can be to attribute the cause more to one's cleverness than to one's luck. But I also know that while governments are often re-elected because of the lack of an alternative, they are invariably defeated regardless of one.

But you can understand the temptations. If you were Robert de Cotret or James Gillies, you would have wanted to believe you unseated a government as much for the wisdom of your economic policy as for the previous dearth of it; or if you were Bill Neville, because of the successful application of your game plan; or if you were Joe Clark, you would have liked to believe that you, too, had some hand in it. Taken together, congratulations were in order all round.

In such an insular mush of sentiment, notions of infallibility flourish. Since you had been so right, the chances were you always would be. When the Clerk of the Privy Council, Michael Pitfield, flew out to Jasper to advise the conquering heroes on the rudiments of changing governments, so dazzled were the members of the new court of conquerers by the lights of their eminence that none could see his way to the airport to meet him. Pitfield, a doomed man, might have done better if he had arrived with a white flag. When he allowed — having been asked what he thought of a two-tiered cabinet — that he saw much against it, his opinion, of course, only clinched the matter. The upper tier of the two-tier cabinet, in its original composition, had no member in it from Toronto, or from British Columbia, or from New Brunswick.

It must have something to do with mountain air, a sense of euphoria induced by lack of oxygen. There certainly is evidence, from both the post-election and the pre-Parliament meetings, that while the scenic wonders of Alberta remain forever exemplary environments for rest and recuperation, they are deadly for the consideration of serious business.

I write this, I confess, not from clippings or from the record, but out of selective memory. Still, it seemed to me, as the new government inched its way towards grasping the levers and nettles of power, that it would have been smarter to have done its prep in Ottawa than in Lotus Land, even allowing for the fact that it was the Prime Minister's own turf.

The trouble with being out there in the seductive ambience of so much scenery and sycophancy is that one so easily believes only what one wants to believe. "Jasper was a disaster," a ranking Tory confessed to me. For out of Jasper (which was the pre-Parliament conclave of the upper-tier of cabinet) came the stubborn resolve that the Tories would stick to their guns — which meant that they were stuck with their platform to assist the home mortgage-holders and to remodel Petro Canada in the image of free enterprise.

Back in June, the cabinet had been sworn in, amid much public and platitudinous regret as to its lack of Quebec timber. Still, the *other* elected member from Quebec, Heward Grafftey, was given a portfolio that defied definition as to responsibility, while another member of the lower tier, Robert Howie, from New Brunswick, was slipped in as a glorified executive assistant to the Minister of Transport. What was missing was anyone with the experience of a George Hees, for one, or an Eldon Woolliams, for another. The Tories, used to eating their young, had now devoured their old.

Even so, it was a more promising cabinet than the one it replaced: David Crombie, Flora MacDonald, David MacDonald, John Crosbie, Elmer Mackay, Don Mazankowski, John Fraser, Ray Hnatyshyn, Ron Atkey — who could not be impressed, watching them take the oath and kiss the Book?

But against that cameo appearance of the many young

lions at Government House at the swearing-in there followed the Prime Minister's news conference with its clangorous note of — well — of a peculiarly petulant defiance. The Tory platform, Joe Clark told the world, was no longer a matter for discussion, but a matter for action. On, then, to Jerusalem!

By then, I think, most of the damage had been done. By then, it became clear, public judgement of the new government was no longer suspended. There would be no honeymoon, not even a handshake, and no outpouring of voter goodwill showed itself in the polls. Instead, even before the Throne Speech, the government began a forced march in retreat of its election promises — about which there was to be no further argument.

That hastily improvised plank in the Tory platform, the promise to move the Canadian embassy from Tel Aviv to Jerusalem, became a hangman's trap, providing the drop for Clark's credibility. The new, young Prime Minister never quite recovered from Jerusalem, that glaring exposure of his innocence, a demonstrated naïveté, which was, it has to be said, made more deadly for the bald political opportunism that was its motivation. Jerusalem hurt, not only because it exposed a weakness, but because it strengthened his enemies.

Further, while Liberals bury their mistakes — in the Senate or beneath a mount of righteous rhetoric — Tories manage to provide them with an eternal life of their own. Witness Jerusalem: rather than saying, as he is now saying, that the embassy move was a mistake — who is not entitled to err? — Clark finessed the issue with an inordinate cleverness. To disengage from a palpable blunder, he sent Robert Stanfield halfway around the world and back. Sure enough, Stanfield returned to confirm the mistake in Joe Clark's campaign promise. Fair enough? No. Clark re-routed Stanfield around the world again, causing Stanfield to become a man in perpetual motion, who served to remind people not only that Joe Clark made a blunder in the campaign of 1979, but how difficult it had become to undo it.

The perambulation of Stanfield — even though undertaken with much dignity and minimal fanfare — *convinced*
Canadians of the seriousness of the mistaken policy, even
many who had thought little about it and were cheerfully
willing to forget it. Far better, one would have thought, for
Clark to have removed the policy early on, and abruptly let it
be forgotten. (Indeed, it was, and remains, so delicate a
domestic political matter that few Liberals have had the nerve
to exploit the folly of it; but Clark has done that for them by
keeping it alive, by putting Stanfield in perpetual motion as a
sort of sandwich-man, bearing a sign that reads "We goofed!")

Jerusalem might have been a useful lesson in humility;
instead, it became an inspiration to defiance. If the advisors
were wrong about Jerusalem — and they were not admitting
it, but merely manipulating the issue — they would hang
tough on PetroCan and on the mortgage deductibility scheme:
they would unite in a determined effort to salvage the platform that had come to represent their personal legitimacy in
the seat of power. More than anything else, they had to assert
not only the wisdom of their platform, but their authority. At
the inner cabinet gathering at Jasper, the advice was "No
more flip-flops."

Rocky Mountain fever!

The question of PetroCan, in the larger context of
energy policy, was symbolic: it was, if nothing else, the only
aspect of the energy issue that the public *thought* it understood
— except only the issue of price. But PetroCan, as a symbol,
grew in importance first of all because the case against
"privatization" was so enormously appealing to common
sense, and secondly because the case for it was profoundly
contradictory to the traditions of Canadian Conservatism.
This contradiction explains why — even at Jasper — the Red
Tories, such as Flora MacDonald and David MacDonald, and
— yes — John Crosbie, were eager to leave PetroCan in place,

while Clark's principal advisors were determined to muscle it into a position that would honour the platform commitment.

And what is the Conservative tradition? I submit that in two of the greatest challenges to nation-building — transportation and communications — the Conservative response was to create a federal agency or instrument, the Canadian National being one and the Canadian Broadcasting Corporation being another. If you like, add to that the establishment by the Conservatives of the central bank. In this most recent example of a national requirement — that of a secured energy supply — it was therefore heretical to the traditions of Canadian Conservatism to abolish the only federal agency with the competence to allow the government of Canada to take an active, interventionist role in national energy policy.

None of this mattered in the spring campaign: most Canadians were hot to defeat Trudeau, and merely bemused by the sight of long lines of motorists queuing at the pumps in the United States. Besides, Clark was promising energy self-sufficiency in a decade's time, not too long to wait for a people who were also told that, if anything, their expectations of the future were not rosy enough. The energy crisis, like unemployment, was something happening to someone else.

But later in the face of the threat, more felt than understood, of substantially increased energy costs for home heat and the family car, PetroCan re-emerged as a symbol of ineptitude. For the average Canadian, feeling an anticipatory shudder, it made as much sense to sell off shares of PetroCan as it would to peddle the Canadian Armoured Corps to Hertz on the eve of a foreign invasion. Nor was it sensible, to the ripe wits and dour philosophers in a thousand morning coffee klatches, to give away half the shares of the corporation to Canadians who believed they already own all of it. No, the policy advisors, struggling to save their pride, fashioned out of this whole issue the worst of achievement — a bad joke.

In August, when the provincial premiers gathered at

Montebello, Bill Davis, the Premier of Ontario, to the aston-
ishment of many, abruptly staked out his case for holding the
line on energy costs. Incredibly, the federal Tories concluded
only that Davis, himself leading a minority government at
Queen's Park, had committed a tactical blunder that would, in
the end, only hurt *him*!

The rationale went something like this: domestic oil
prices had to rise to something closer to OPEC prices (this in
the name of simple equity for the oil-producing provinces);
further, the public was prepared for and were willing to pay
more now, in the interest of equity — and of conservation —
and as a price for eventual self-sufficiency. Davis, then, was
grandstanding, and — we'd all see — when the deal was made
with Alberta, and the coming federal budget gave the promise
of fiscal responsibility at long last, Canadians, Ontarians
among them, would wonder why all the fuss. In short, while
Davis was playing politics, the feds were practising states-
manship. And in the end, having taken the plunge to hold
back on the rate of oil price increases, Davis — not Clark —
would have painted himself in a corner. He might, in fact,
even be defeated in a provincial election.

But let us examine some features of this strange and
aloof attitude, this looking-down-the-nose from Ottawa at
the man who had, in many minds, done more to give Clark his
opportunity than any other politician, save only Trudeau
himself. Clark had, after all, won his plurality in Davis's
Ontario. In a province with ninety-five seats in Parliament,
the Tories had taken fifty-six, and most of those in Ontario's
industrial heartland.

One would therefore expect the Clark government, in
shaping its energy policy, to take note of Ontario, the source
of such a large part of its mandate. Instead they set their heart
on a policy of self-determination, and ultimately self-destruc-
tion. The problem as they saw it was how to finesse past
Ontario an oil-pricing policy that would satisfy Alberta.

Given that Alberta's position on pricing was, rudely put, the higher the better, and Ontario's was the cheaper the better, the designated victim was certain to be Davis. One would have thought that the principal component in that consideration would have been the opposite: what is the optimum price that Ontario would pay to Alberta? But no, it was the other way around.

In this inversion of political strategy, the government was relying on a set of assumptions that proved to be serious miscalculations:

—that the federal government had time on its side;
—that so long as Trudeau remained leader the minority government was safe (and even safer once Trudeau announced his plans to retire);
—that Davis would have a provincial election to face in Ontario before there was a federal election;
—that, all the above being true, Davis therefore needed Clark more than Clark needed Davis, and that once the energy policy pill had been swallowed by Ontario the feds would then see what they could do to repair the injured relations with their provincial cousins;
—that there was, above all, *time.*

Well, all the above turned out to be wrong. More important, Ontario did the finessing: Davis showed his hand early, even while the federal policy was somewhere between gestation, resolution, and negotiation.

Looked at from Queen's Park, there were three motivating reasons for the seeming haste to air Ontario's position. The first of these, of course, was that the federal policy was simply wrong, that it was not only bad economics but deadly politics. Reason enough, you might say, but there was yet more.

The second and third reasons involve some of the Davis personnel — such as Hugh Segal and Les Horswill in the policy and priorities secretariat, both of whom had served with Robert Stanfield in Ottawa, circa 1972-74. They knew, from that experience, the perils to Ontario of Clark's unfolding policy but, more, the perils to any party of having none at all. You could ask Bob Stanfield. At year end, 1973, the minority Trudeau government stood lower in the public opinion poll than any Canadian government had in Gallup's history (until Clark's) — nineteen points behind the Conservatives. It was in the winter of 1973 when energy first emerged as a crisis issue. During that winter and the early spring, while the Grits developed a policy response, the Tory caucus remained deadlocked between the opposing views of its western members and its Ontario members. When the government fell, or allowed itself to fall, Stanfield felt his party's failure to achieve a coherent energy policy had already lost the election. He still does: so does Segal. The issue of wage and price controls did not lose the election; the Tories had already lost it.

And, finally, the people around Davis had little use for the people around Clark. It was not that their relations were not cordial, friendly, even frank — but that those at Queen's Park had no confidence in the political judgement of their opposite numbers in Ottawa. What was hardest to bear, in the debate over energy policy between Ottawa and Queen's Park, was the realization that the feds weren't *listening!*

So, the provincial Tories took a poll. Even better, they hired Allan Gregg, the federal Tory party's in-house pollster, to conduct the poll. Gregg's survey examined three questions: the state of Clark's popularity in Ontario at the time; the make-up of Clark's Ontario vote in the federal election; and finally, the sensitivity of the energy issue in the province.

The findings confirmed what most of Davis's advisors profoundly believed. First, that the federal government — and Clark — were already in trouble with the Ontario voters; second, that Clark's vote in the federal election had come largely from the hard core of Davis supporters; and finally, that energy — the cost of it — was now the major concern of the electorate.

The provincial Tories, who paid for the poll, asked only that Gregg furnish the relevant data to his Ottawa client, which he did. It failed to impress.

Horswill was even dispatched to Ottawa to brief the Ontario members of the Tory federal caucus on Ontario's position and warn them of the likely consequences of the proposed federal policy. He was given a rough ride. Curiously, the principal reason for supporting the federal policy was ideological. The time had come, Horswill was told, to get the government out of the energy marketplace, to allow the free enterprise system to work out the price, supply, and demand for oil. Ontario, someone said to Horswill, was only being "parochial" — the rest of the country would support Clark.

And so it seemed at the subsequent first ministers' conference at which Davis, speaking for Ontario, was visibly isolated in his stand. There was, afterwards, a good deal of clucking sympathy expressed for Davis by the Clark people. As it turned out, they might better have saved it for themselves.

What followed, with the defeat of the budget in the House, was the fall of a government which was never to have the opportunity to demonstrate its worth. In summary, it was a tragedy of miscalculation.

By failing to call Parliament sooner than it did, the government insulated itself in a political vacuum of its own making. Since it heard no opposition, it saw none.

By assuming that it could not be defeated, it was prepared to run enormous political risks. The miscalculation was not so much one of arrogance as of innocence. It failed to comprehend the swiftness with which cynicism, opportunism, and an abiding lust for power could combine to revive a defeated Liberal Party and even resurrect its leadership.

Somewhere, in the cosmos, Machiavelli and Mackenzie King are shaking hands.

Northwood,
New Brunswick.
January 9, 1980.

Introduction

When the first Conservative federal government of Canada in sixteen years, the Joe Clark government of 1979, self-immolated less than seven months after its election, it left a number of questions behind:

—Why did Parliament self-destruct? Was Canada's thirty-first federal general election really necessary?

—What were Joe Clark's policies, anyway, on PetroCan, on interest rates, on a "stimulative deficit," on external relations, and the Canadian embassy in Israel?

—What kind of fellow was Clark? How did he behave when he was unbuttoned? Was he ever unbuttoned? Was he his own man?

Canadian voters, who thought they'd made their choice back on May 22, 1979, were faced with the need to do it again, and maybe again and again, as it now seemed, "until you get it right." But rational choices require some understanding. This book is an attempt to make sense of the shards of carnival mirror left from the wreckage of the circus that Canada's twenty-first government became before its end.

Well, as Agatha Christie's admirable detective Hercule Poirot was fond of observing, the facts do have a way of "arranging themselves." What follows is such an arrangement; it is a filtered, edited examination of the life of the Joe Clark government of 1979 from its genesis to its untimely death, gleaned from Hansard and newspaper, radio, T.V., and periodical coverage; taken from every press release and speech text issued by every department administered by the Clark government; supplemented by conversations with Clark-watchers, civil servants, Clark colleagues, journalists, paper-shredders, and cleaning staff. It is an attempt to put the 1979 Clark administration into context — or maybe to find if it had a context.

A word about the filtering and editing. Both, obviously, have been done according to the truth as I saw it, with the benefit of hindsight. Both necessarily involve the elimination of events, people, and statements that seemed less than essential. Editorial judgements are ever subjective. I've no apology for that; but it deserves passing mention, however obvious it may be.

A lot of what follows will be critical of the Clark administration. That's natural. Since only parties in power can act, only they are subject to scrutiny of policy. That's a lesson hard-learned (if ever) by governments. Surrounded by critics, they see themselves besieged, attacked on every side. I decided years ago that the best measure of the maturity and civilization of any politician was the time lapse between his or her assuming office and the development of the bunker mentality. For most, that progression occupies a depressingly brief span of time. A couple of examples, if I may digress:

—In 1965, hardly comfortable yet in his East Block office on Parliament Hill, Prime Minister Lester Pearson used up most of a full cabinet meeting instructing his ministers that none of them was *ever* to appear on a CBC program called *This Hour Has Seven Days* without Pearson's explicit permission. The show was "out to get us," warned the Prime Minister. (Interestingly, less than ninety minutes after that meeting ended, two of the Pearson Cabinet phoned the *Seven Days* office in Toronto to tell us about it; both of them were on the next program in the series, without Mike Pearson's prior blessing.)

—In 1978 a senior member of then Prime Minister Trudeau's staff, asked to produce Mr. Trudeau for a CBC television interview which had been promised, snarled, "Why should we help you bastards? All the CBC does is try to make this government look bad."

The point is simply that governments, which live at ground zero, collect all the comment and criticism around; it goes with the turf — but that doesn't mean it does not smart. So some, understandably, bite back. And that's fair, too.

So, if most of the critical comments in this book, inferred or direct, are aimed at the Clark government, that's because this is a book *about* the Clark government.

Personal bias? Well, as a private individual I've voted for three of our federal political parties, and as a journalist I've been dropped on from a considerable height by five (Liberal, Progressive Conservative, NDP/CCF, Social Credit, Communist.)

My only public office is and has been as a member of the Toronto Board of Health, an august body to which I was appointed by Toronto City Council. Although my appointment was unanimously approved (another candidate turned out to live outside the city's boundaries) I'm told I was a candidate of the "reform wing" of council, whatever that means.

People who tell lies, even if they are in public office, make me vomit; hypocrisy makes me angry; pomposity makes me snicker. I do not believe that pain in any way makes the human spirit more noble; but I do have a notion that most public oxen should be administered a regular goring, just to keep them alert.

Now, briefly, a word about how this all got done: Unhappily there are many contributors whom I dare not thank for their own peace of mind. But I do. Jill Troyer, a young journalist who constantly makes me fear for the viability of us older folks, provided research aid beyond description or adequate thanks. Glenys Moss made it possible.

The fascinating thing about politics, the most empiric and existential of all human pursuits, is the process. It was as an examination of the bliss and fatuity of that process that this book was begun long before anyone knew it would be dealing with the first *and last* 200 days of Clark's 1979 government. Ben Bradlee of the Washington *Post* defined journalism as "history on the run." I hope these rough-notes-for-history will encourage other, more scholarly, works in the near future.

~ 1 ~

Jasper: The Seeds of Dissolution

The seeds of the dissolution of Canada's twenty-first government were sown in the soft, mountain air at Jasper, Alberta, when, in August of 1979, the cabinet repaired to the cloud-high railway spa for spiritual refreshment and the pragmatic horse-trading of *réal politique*. Before the cabinet had finished its deliberations the fledgling government's power brokers were clearly identified; the cabinet's "Red Tories" were on notice that they remained chiefly on sufferance; and the early and unequivocal defeat of the government had been fore-ordained. The CNR had been paid for the accommodation, but it was the country that would pick up the tab, three months later, when the course established in Jasper led in a direct line to the success of the NDP want-of-confidence motion in the feisty December House of Commons.

In Jasper in August, no one considered early defeat possible. As all politicians know, minority governments are rarely brought down easily; they must virtually *court* defeat. In the

British system, to which Canada is heir, Parliaments (even those housing minority governments) defeat the party in power only when two circumstances are woven together: the opposition parties must sense an issue of principle on which they disagree with the government, or at least an issue which they believe saleable to the electorate as one of principle; and the opposition must be *in a mood* to destroy the government. That second imperative, that aura of bloody-mindedness, is the barometer most closely watched by every seasoned parliamentary observer. The temper of the house, as it's often called, is still and always has been the major factor governing the life and death of minority governments. Rationality, even personal survival and vested self-interest, have no claims on the votes of the honourable members when their dander is raised and their blood heated; no doberman ever showed the dedication for the jugular evinced by a pack of opposition M.P.s lusting for a taste of blood from the Treasury Benches. Defeat of minority government can come only when opposition benches are supplied both with the motive and the will. The fledgling Clark administration unknowingly sowed the seeds of both criteria the fourth week of August 1979, in its Jasper cabinet meetings.

The Prime Minister had chosen Jasper as the location of his meetings to permit reflective evaluation of policy and programs away from the Ottawa centrifuge (and away from the civil service mandarins who were still suspected of Liberal contamination by the Tory new boys). It was in Jasper that he was determined to arrange the order of business of Canada's twenty-first government. Having arranged to delay meeting the House of Commons longer after his election than any previous Canadian Prime Minister, Joe Clark was determined to get it right, off the top. Policy directions would be set, cabinet solidarity welded, legislation presaged and budgets foreshadowed. Jasper would be the loins and viscera of Canada's twenty-first government ministry; the strength of

Rocky Mountain granite and the purity of glacial ice-water would infuse the Throne Speech of 1979. It was only right — and fair.

Not everything surrounding the events of August 26 to August 30, 1979, was Wagnerian, of course. There were those several members of the cabinet and advisory staff who found the mountain spring waters less than satisfying and incurred remarkable tabs in the many-splendoured bars of the CNR hostelry. One cabinet minister, the Honourable William Jarvis, Minister of Urban Affairs, arrived at the cabinet chalet sporting an impressive limp one morning; he left shortly, and returned by RCMP cruiser clad in an impressive ankle cast and mounted on borrowed crutches. "I fell off the sidewalk last night," he explained to reporters. No one expressed surprise. The lodge staff, too, was less than universally speechless at the honour bestowed them. One waitress was seen leaving the Moose's Nook Restaurant in tears after serving a sumptuous dinner to the Prime Minister and his party of a dozen-odd. Asked to explain, another waitress said the rather boisterous group had been substantially more demanding than most clients, and had left the room without leaving even a nickel's tip for the waitress — shades of budgets to come.

And there was the press: members of the Ottawa gallery found their treatment at the Jasper Summit somewhat more well-intentioned than effectual. Clark press aides were delighted, for example, to move a press conference outside, on the suggestion of T.V. film crews, to take advantage of the gorgeous mountain backdrop; but they positioned the press table so as to negate the beauty of the scenery. The Prime Minister had also, as it turned out, taken two excellent and popular press aides to Jasper, in the persons of Jock Osler and Art Lyons; both, unfortunately, were unilingual anglophones. Two well-liked francophone press aides had been left to mind the home fires in Ottawa; and French reporters in Jasper, representing CBC's Radio Canada as well as Quebec French-language newspapers, were left to translate press releases from English and stew in their own Gallic juices. (This from the staff of a Prime Minister who spoke French in Alberta more frequently than his francophone predecessor. The new P.M. had, beyond doubt, been skewered by his own staff, no small matter for a federal leader bleeding for enough Quebec members to count on the fingers of one hand.)

But it was policy that Jasper was to be about, and policy that was discussed in the pleasant cottage just down the (treacherous) sidewalk from the main lodge. Policy was to be clean, simple, and brutal. The new government would rule Parliament, and *rule* was the operative word, "as though we had a majority." Moreover, as Joe Clark told those assembled: "If we don't live up to our promises, we're dead."

There was the question of *which* promises: those of the dear, lost, carefree days of the spring campaign — "stimulative deficits," and a pox on those asking Canadians to lower their expectations — or those of the oppressive weeks of summer — retrenchment, high interest rates, and hard-times-brought-on-by-Liberal-extravagance? Lowell Murray, the Prime Minister's chief advisor, who sat in his easy chair situated unobtrusively in the corner of the cottage living room, won the day with his bulky Green Book, Tory Writ in a hard-covered binder as thick as the Metro Toronto telephone book. It was to be hard lines all the way. Truth is more cruel than campaign euphoria. The daffodils were clear losers to the Treasury thunderheads.

The Clark cabinet was determined to do away with the nagging problems of image and semantics that had plagued it all summer. One memorable cabinet meeting had devoted an inordinate period to discussion of alternate words to describe their goal of "privatizing" PetroCan. Aware from a barrage of nasty comment that, whatever the merits of their proposal, the concept of "privatize" wouldn't sell, the cabinet considered the appropriate "real" word to reflect their intention: "de-nationalize." Many thousands of cabinet words later, it was agreed that de-nationalize sounded too strong. So, semantic purists to the contrary, privatize it was, and privatize it would remain.

But the real semantic block troubling the loafer-and-sweater cabinet at Jasper hung on a phrase that had begun to surface in the late summer, as the new government abandoned one campaign policy after another. As Joe Clark and John Crosbie played Pontius Pilate on Parliament Hill, washing their hands of just about every pledge made in April and May, someone applied the term "flip-flops" to Tory government policy. The Prime Minister's Office was deeply wounded and aggrieved.

Flip-flop? No government, surely, could endure an epithet so easily remembered by an electorate, no matter how malleable. It was, after all, only two syllables; worse even than "fuddle-duddle." Clearly not tolerable. From now on it was to be hard lines all the way.

The "hard-line" program consisted chiefly of two parts: a determination to proceed with the dismantling of PetroCan, a project probably first born in the breast of the Prime Minister, and clearly one dear to him, and the introduction of a get-tough budget. Ironically, John Crosbie, the Finance Minister who proved such a loyal good-soldier in the dismal days of December, was not a hard-liner at Jasper. The economic policies came, not from Crosbie, but from Jim Gillies and Robert de Cotret; one a failed Tory candidate on May 22, and the other an ex-M.P. — and both men with easy and regular access to the prime ministerial ear.

The fifty-five-year-old Jim Gillies, with a doctorate in economics and a teaching career behind him, had been twice elected in the Toronto riding of Don Valley, in 1972 and again in 1974. An Air Force veteran and a former chairman of the Ontario Economic Council, Gillies was regarded as a hard-liner on the Jerusalem embassy move. During the campaign, while Lowell Murray had anguished from Ottawa over Joe Clark's startling decision to move Canada's Israeli embassy from Tel Aviv to the Holy City, Gillies and Bill Neville, travelling with the P.C. leader on his plane, were believed the men who kept Clark's resolve firm on that issue. Gillies, said to have a knack for seizing on the best bits of Clark rhetoric and ignoring the rest, was, of all the leader's staff, the one best at stroking the future P.M., and the one who most frequently made him laugh, a quality greatly esteemed by Clark.

Bob de Cotret, at thirty-five, was a whiz-kid economist. Had he achieved the Ottawa riding victory most expected him to manage handily in May, de Cotret would probably have been in John Crosbie's uncomfortable shoes; but one couldn't have a Finance Minister in the Senate, unavailable for opposition questions, unable even to present his budget on the floor of the House; so the over-achieving young economist had to settle for the Senate appointment and the Ministry of Trade and Economic Development. Gillies was widely regarded as an intellectual gadfly, witty, urbane, sophisticated, and maybe a bit lazy. By contrast, de Cotret was the ultra-disciplined, uptight whirlwind; he'd been on Richard Nixon's staff of economic advisors at thirty, and president of the prestigious Conference Board of Canada at thirty-two. No one accused de Cotret of humour, but no one denied his drive, his dedication, or his influence with the leader.

Now the real perimeters of power had been drawn. Joe Clark probably owed his job to Flora MacDonald as much as to any one person: at the 1976 leadership convention both had pledged themselves to support the other in event either was clearly knocked out of the running; but it was Flora's instant and unhesitating walk across the Ottawa Civic Centre auditorium that clearly had swung a critical balance to "everybody's second choice." And Flora had been rewarded with that plum of cabinet portfolios, External Affairs, the

first Canadian (indeed, Commonwealth) woman so honoured. Flora, though, was known as a "Red Tory," along with Health Minister David Crombie (the erstwhile tiny-perfect-mayor of Toronto) and Secretary of State David MacDonald. The three, it's related, were appalled by the Jasper mind-set; equally clearly, they lost.

Flora MacDonald and her Red Tory supporters (David Crombie, David MacDonald, John Crosbie) wanted to forget the whole PetroCan scheme. The Tories had managed to skate the platform plank past an electorate more concerned with punishing Pierre Trudeau than with electing Joe Clark, during a balmy spring. But what would happen, for example, during some possible future *winter* campaign, when voters might see PetroCan as a touchstone of security against their fears of freezing in the dark. The Red Tories lost; and they lost again on the economic debate. It was to be stick-it-to-them time come the first session of Parliament in October, and no questions asked — or answered.

The winners were clear. Along with key strategist Lowell Murray and aides Gillies and Neville, they were the cabinet tough guys, Robert de Cotret and Sinclair Stevens, and behind them, the serried ranks of small *c* Conservatives, crowding their coat tails and basking in their reflected glory. Only two months before, Lowell Murray, Progressive Conservative campaign chairman in the 1979 election campaign, had vowed to a reporter that he would never return to a job in Ottawa. He'd won, after all; there were no further peaks to scale. And he'd won, in his own words, by "leaving as little to chance as possible."

But now, on his advice and with the support of Treasury Board Chairman Stevens and the rest, the Clark government was about to hazard everything on a colossal bluff. Persuaded the Canadian economy needed a purgative, the new cabinet was going to bank everything on the gut conviction that the opposition parties would be terrified of an early election for a number of valid reasons: First, over a score of Liberal M.P.s could only secure decent parliamentary pensions if they survived in their employment until April 1980. Second, Pierre Trudeau was, within ninety days, to announce his impending retirement as Liberal leader. ("We're home free," crowed a Tory M.P. "They won't dare defeat us until after their leadership convention in March. We've got a blank cheque. We can do any goddamned thing we like.") Third, too, the bony rump of Quebec-based Social Credit M.P.s wanted to cling to their seats so long as that was respectable.

The Clark government, therefore, reasoned they could do any damned thing they wished in their first year. There would be time for the electoral goodies next year, or the year after. Moreover, if stymied by the obstruction of the opposition, the new government would *force* its way upon a reluctant House of Commons. They were too impatient for seduction.

But what the Conservatives had misjudged was "the temper of the house." Just as in the finely tuned tradition of British jurisprudence, justice must be seen to be done, so in Parliament, honourable members must not *be seen* to be bullied. Being bullied, they knew, couldn't be explained to the home folks, nor lived with over drinks or dinner in the Grill Room of the Chateau Laurier. Few fish have so little pride as to bite, in the presence of their peers, on a bare, steel hook.

But it was only cold steel the Tory cabinet offered the House of Commons in November when, intent on "keeping our promises," the government threatened to end debate on a bill to offer Canadians tax relief from mortgage interest by imposing closure on Parliament. (The Liberals had imposed closure, a device to artificially end a debate, often themselves. But they had learned that the Parliamentary guillotine could cut both ways when the House erupted over a closure motion. In 1957, it had sent Prime Minister St. Laurent to the country and John Diefenbaker to the head of a new government.) Parliament wasn't quite ready to defeat the government over closure when the Tory threat appeared, but it did help establish the mood that led to the eventual fall. Like boys and girls in any other playpen, M.P.s find it difficult to endure public humiliation. The art of compromise founders on such emotional trivialities.

There was irony to spare in the Clark government threats to use closure in Parliament. In 1956, a Grade Eleven student from High River, Alberta, Charles Joseph Clark, had won a Rotary Club public-speaking scholarship, an award which carried as a prize a trip to Ottawa. Young Joe Clark spent his Ottawa visit sitting in the public gallery of the House of Commons and waiting patiently to meet three Tory heroes of the time: National P.C. Leader George Drew, prairie Lochinvar John Diefenbaker, and the doyen of the Alberta Tory establishment, Senator Donald Cameron. Joe Clark saw a part of the extraordinary pipeline debate of 1956, a debate that eventually toppled the St. Laurent government. He saw a complacent Liberal government invoking closure to force its legislation through a recalcitrant House; and on his return to High River he told his mother that Canada "didn't have democracy." The opposition in Parliament, he felt, had to be stronger. The brilliant Grade Eleven, High River debater and orator didn't like closure — in 1956. But that was before the first taste of power, the first infusion of royal jelly, the first seductive intimation of all there was to manipulate, or to lose. It was, in Dalton Camp's memorable description, before Joe Clark discovered ambition "in some corner of his mind, like a winning lottery ticket."

It seemed, in the brief life of the 1979 Parliament, that the government, listening only to the siren calls of macho policy and power politics, had become tone deaf to the alarm bells that are essential to every parliamentarian. So hard line it was; closure it was to be.

Storm warnings followed. External Affairs Minister Flora MacDonald was Europe-bound on government business.

Tradition has that on such occasions opposition parties accord an absent Secretary of State for External Affairs a "pair" in the House of Commons. (Pairing is a system by which an absent member arranges with a member in the party opposite to abstain from a recorded vote during that absence; it is a common parliamentary courtesy, and one extended automatically, until December, 1979, to ministers sent abroad on government affairs.) But this time the pair was refused; the Liberals wouldn't promise to have a member stand down from any recorded vote. The Clark government paid no heed. Flora went to Paris and the twenty-first government went up the spout.

There was still time for survival. The therapy offered by the Crosbie budget of December 13 was pure poison to the opposition parties — adding principle to the motivation amply supplied already by threats of closure and chronic delusions of adequacy from a government balanced on the knife-edge of defeat. But even after the budget speech and irresistible evidence the House was of a mind to destroy itself, the government could have survived.

All the government needed do, even at the penultimate moment of its destruction, was to revert to a previous order of business. After the budget speech was read and reported on December 13, 1979, the Clark regime could have announced a decision to postpone the budget debate (and the fatal want-of-confidence motions) while it carried on with other business. It could then have introduced, for example, the Freedom of Information Act and a series of other measures popular with the media and voters. By the time those bills had passed and the budget debate resumed, say in January, the electoral ardour of M.P.s might have cooled. Perusal of virtuous bills passed in the interim might have persuaded Liberal and New Democratic M.P.s they didn't particularly want to run against, say, a shiny new Freedom of Information Act; the government might very likely have survived and lived to fight another day, some other year.

In fact, the government had developed just such a game plan, and discussed it before External Affairs Minister Mac-Donald left for Paris. After introducing the budget, it was agreed that the government would suspend debate on the budget; it would then press forward with the bill to give Canadians tax relief from mortgage interest, the bill the Liberals had been filibustering. The Grits might go on fighting the measure, but they sure as hell wouldn't force a general election over the one economic *goody* that had survived from the Tory campaign platform. Freedom of information could follow; Jed Baldwin, who'd championed the measure from the start, had a substantial, indeed an almost unanimous, press backing for his views. Who would defeat a government over *that?*

Flora left for France certain all was under control. No one was more surprised when the government allowed debate to proceed on the budget, with introduction of the fatal want-of-confidence motions.

Never mind. There was still a fall-back position. The Social Credit could easily be wiped out in a new election. Their Quebec base had shrunk alarmingly; they'd already swallowed the Clark refusal to grant them formal party status in the House, with the loss of all the perks that represented. They would bite down one more time. Of course they would. In fact, until less than sixty minutes before the final vote, the Tory front benches still expected the Socred members to support them. They were *there,* for God's sake! Why in the world would they even be present in the Centre Block if they didn't mean to vote? They had to be allowed to complete their sulk; but they'd vote. They didn't want a winter election, either.

Mind you, with Flora trapped in Paris, even the Socred votes would give the government only a tied result — if all the Liberals showed up, which was unlikely. But that was okay, too. Because in the event of a tie during a roll-call vote in Parliament, the Speaker of the House has the right and responsibility of casting the deciding vote. And that would be dandy for at least two reasons.

First, any Speaker may respectably tell the House that he does not feel it should be *his* vote, as arbiter of their proceedings, that plunges the country into a general election campaign. Some opposition M.P.s, especially the Speaker's Liberal colleagues, mightn't like that rationale a lot, but it was not one with which they could take violent public issue.

Second, the present Speaker, the Honourable James Alexander Jerome, the Sudbury attorney and former alderman in that city, need not fear for the need to campaign in Sudbury's frigid winter. An *arrangement*, quite a respectable arrangement (one would not apply the word "deal" for a Speaker of Parliament), had been made when Mr. Jerome assumed his august position in October. Indeed, in the best juridical tradition, it was even an arrangement with a precedent.

Mr. Jerome's predecessor, the Honourable Lucien Lamoureux, had, like Jerome, hankered for appointment as a *permanent* speaker of the House of Commons. Pierre Trudeau, like Mike Pearson before him, had refused that boon. But Mr. Lamoureux had been persuaded to serve anyway, from January 18, 1966, until September 30, 1974, with the promise that, on his retirement as Speaker, whether by choice or electoral defeat, he would be given a government appointment either as a judge or a member of Canada's diplomatic corps. To make the deal binding, the assent of the leader of the opposition, Robert Stanfield, was sought and obtained. So no matter who won the next election, the Cornwall lawyer would not be unemployed. And it was to be so. In 1974, having chosen not to run again in that election, the Speaker abdicated and was appointed Canada's Ambassador to Luxemburg, a rewarding but not too taxing diplomatic post.

Lucien Lamoureux was, in 1979, able to view the death of the new Clark government from Luxemburg with a certain comfortable detachment.

Did James Jerome have the same sort of guarantee? The government was defeated on December 13, 1979, and the House dissolved on December 14. Just six days later, barely tucked back into his Sudbury home, the Speaker of the House was reported by Canadian Press to have announced he would not be a candidate in the new election. He had hoped the late, lamented Parliament would find time to debate a permanent speakership, said Mr. Jerome. That had not proved possible. However, the Clark government, through the office of the Prime Minister, would shortly be announcing a federal appointment for the Speaker. Since the nature of his new duties would be announced soon by Joe Clark, it would not be "proper" for him to describe them at this time.

The tooth fairy finally found James Jerome's Sudbury address January 4, 1980. Mr. Jerome wasn't home. Using up one of the last perks of the job he'd quit, Mr. Jerome was in Cyprus; there the former House Speaker was observing the January Mediterranean while attending the annual meetings of the Commonwealth Speakers' Association.

Gift parcels were being accepted during Mr. Jerome's absence, however. This one, unwrapped at an Ottawa press conference by Joe Clark, made James Jerome associate chief justice of the Federal Court of Canada. A reasonable job and one with prospects: the man bumped upstairs to the job of chief justice was Arthur Thurlow (a former Liberal member of the Nova Scotia legislature) who was sixty-six years of age.

Mr. Clark said he would never have made such an appointment "solely as a political reward"; he had consulted with Pierre Trudeau about the appointment, he said. The Prime Minister added that such appointments were in tune with a "long standing practice." As evidence he cited the example of Lucien Lamoureux.

So, even though (for reasons shrouded in the mists of Joe Clark's intellectual, decision-making apparatus) the government had done a private and unpublicized flip-flop on its avowed intention to avoid the budget motions entirely, things would still be okay. The Socreds would come around, however shamefacedly, and the Speaker would save the day, the government, and the Parliament.

Not perhaps privy to the finely tuned calculations of the government's front benches, the New Democratic Party, too, believed the Clark regime would survive. Like de Cotret, Stevens, Clark, and the rest, the New Democrats thought it inconceivable the Grits would force an election while leaderless. (One NDP M.P. realizing in the members' lobby before the vote that *all* the Liberals — hearty, halt or lame — were assembled to vote, stammered in amazement. "You guys are out of your fucking minds," he expostulated with somewhat less than parliamentary propriety.)

Anyhow, the New Democrats reasoned, the Tories were right about one thing: the Socreds would vote and would sustain the government.

All of those theories, however, were, as the systems engineers say, disfunctional. The morning after John Crosbie's budget speech, Joe Clark's staff laboured on a graceful peroration for the Prime Minister to deliver if the government actually fell. But no one in the PMO believed it would happen. True, the five Social Credit members had said they would abstain from the vote on the New Democratic want-of-confidence motion; true, the Prime Minister had disdained hints from the Socred M.P.s that their support could be wooed, even won, by amelioration of the harsh, new fuel taxes in the Crosbie budget for their hard-pressed rural Quebec constituents.

But it wouldn't happen. Too many Liberal M.P.s wanted those April pension guarantees; and the Grits, after all, had a "lame duck" leader. (After the vote one Liberal told a T.V.

camera, "Better a lame duck leader than a turkey for a Prime Minister.") The Socreds were fearful of losing the tiny base they'd clung to in May; they would come around. The Grits were fearful, period. They'd see that a few members missed the recorded vote in the unlikely event the Social Credit caucus actually refused to sustain the government. Lowell Murray had been right; Bob de Cotret had been right; the Prime Minister *was* right.

But the Social Credit M.P.s, their spines stiffened (if they needed it) by repeated administrations of Tory steel, did abstain. Flora, summoned from Paris, missed the Concorde to New York by ten minutes. (Not that it mattered; with no Socred support, the government had lost, by the numbers, before the combined weight of Liberal and New Democratic votes bent the Prime Minister's head over his prepared text of farewell.) It remained only for Joe Clark to visit the Governor General the following morning, obtain leave to call an election and inform the House, immediately thereafter that it had been dissolved. Lowell Murray, who had returned from a Maritime fishing trip to become Joe Clark's constant companion on Parliament Hill, may have thought back on his proud boast before the 1979 election that the campaign was "controlled."

The government, too, for its brief life, was controlled. The difficulty was that, just as election campaigns are controlled only to the degree that voters, too, are controlled, so with government. A controlled government isn't a helluva lot of use when the House of Commons is hell-bent for dissolution.

The question is: how did the House get there? Thinking of an election call within seven months, most Canadian Clark-watchers in May 1979 would have supplied the Irish injunction that, "You can't get there from here." But we did, with — and maybe for — a vengeance.

~ 2 ~

Joe Clark: A Profile

Joe Clark may have been the first Canadian Prime Minister who seemed smaller than life-sized. A radio reporter, seeking the P.C. leader at a shopping plaza rally in April of 1979, walked right by the future Prime Minister and had to be directed back to him. "I thought he was much shorter," she said. For a man topping six feet, Joe Clark has a remarkable ability to melt into his background.

Dalton Camp, one of two Canadian political observers able to perform major verbal surgery without the loss of a drop of blood (Stephen Lewis is the other), put the case with lethal eloquence in his book *Points of Departure*: "Clark is a hard man to find in a crowd; his magnetic field is small, aura has not yet encompassed him . . . he is easily lost. . . . Head waiters, from the Chateau Laurier Grill Room to the Louis IX would have been inclined to seat him by the kitchen door." (In truth, on his first date with his then secretary, Maureen McTeer, at the end of 1972, Clark was patronized by the wine steward at the Louis IX in Hull and, after dinner, lost his way back to Ottawa. His biographer, David L. Humphreys, explains that an RCMP constable, spotting the new M.P.'s Alberta licence plates, directed him home.)

Like Robert Stanfield before him, Joe Clark often failed to project a genuinely keen wit or a delight in the ridiculous. The emergence of televised Question Periods in the House of Commons in October of 1977, however, coincided with a more confident Joe Clark, willing to rely on the "head notes" he'd been uneasy about earlier and to trade barbs with the Liberal front benches. It is clear, in hindsight, that the video-tape clips of the best of the Question Period carried on network newscasts did a lot to build Clark's credibility as the "alternate leader" — a description he'd cribbed from Alberta Premier Peter Lougheed. But viewers for the full Question Period telecasts were as few as regular readers of Hansard. So for many Canadians, even as the 1979 election campaign began, the gag line, "Joe who?" still represented a respectable question.

Ironically, the bad joke of the 1979 campaign reflected a bit of Clark campaign literature from twelve years earlier. In his first run for public office, Clark had come astonishingly close to whipping Arthur Dixon, Alberta's Social Credit Speaker of the Legislature, in Calgary South. Spreading the word in that 1967 Alberta general election campaign, the twenty-eight-year-old Clark approved a flyer intended to make him better known to Calgary voters. It was headed: "What'sajoeclark?" That campaign flyer was, by 1979, a highly treasured collector's memento.

Charles Joseph Clark is, first and forever, a paint-by-numbers politician; a self-constructed, artfully crafted party leader, he fabricated himself from the disappointments of experience and the failures of ambition. Always deliberate, always happy to be underestimated by opponents, Clark was, from his first political forays, a formidable adversary. In his youth, writes Dalton Camp, "Clark concealed his lack of sophistication beneath a cloak of gravity." By 1979, Camp was writing of a party leader "who is elevating the art of politics to a science. While there is no magic in Clark," wrote the Tory poet laureate, "there is much method." By the campaign of 1979, Joe Clark had even taught himself the habits of spontaneity; he would join in a singsong on his campaign plane, wine glass in hand, face alight with pleasure at the fellowship of the press entourage. One press cynic said after his election that Clark's 9 A.M. Friday morning press conferences could always be predicted by the sound of prime ministerial laughter floating two blocks down Ottawa's Wellington Street, from the Langevin Block to the National Press Building. It was, he said, always a solid "haw-haw." Very healthy, natural, and loud. Nothing like the hysterical giggle that had occasionally betrayed the dark imperatives behind John Diefenbaker's amusements and discomfitures.

Clark is a morning person. After his election in 1979, he surprised reporters by arriving at his office near eight every morning; the open government he'd promised negated by his turning up for work before T.V. camera crews were ready for their first "photo opportunity" of the day. (Trudeau had rarely appeared before 9:30 or 10:00 A.M. But the Liberal P.M. had been a great one for evening work; not so Joe Clark, who also, as it soon developed, liked a Churchillian nap after lunch.) Even when Joe Clark announced his candidacy for the Tory leadership in Montreal, after having announced it in Edmonton the previous day, his press conference was called for 11 A.M.; Joe's French was better before lunch, when he was rested, than in the afternoons.

By 1979, too, Clark had begun to look ever so slightly like a young John A. Macdonald: a bit lanky, teetering slightly on his heels, arms akimbo or (worst of all for his appearance) hands resting on hips, tummy thrust comfortably forward under a slightly straining belt. (All of this perhaps is a legacy of earnest advice received in 1974 from a former Dalhousie University classmate who'd watched Clark in action during the election campaign: "Try to speak without too much activity with your hands, which are long and skinny and convey something of a Diefenbaker impression.")

Joe Clark is nothing if not a learner. Early Alberta campaigns taught him the New Democratic Party techniques of door-knocking canvasses; Peter Lougheed taught him to run as an "alternate," but never as an "opposition" candidate; George Hees, running a campaign seminar in Clark's Edmonton student days, read the lesson: never leave anyone with apparent willingness; have someone else drag you away. Clark had the Attorney General of Alberta "drag him" from meetings throughout the P.C. federal leadership convention of February 1976.

When the High River boy came swinging in from deep left field to capture the 1976 leadership convention on its third ballot, he'd already had four years in Parliament and fifteen years in active politics. Joe Clark in 1976 was a cross between the Six-Million Dollar Man and Mrs. Malaprop; one moment dazzling with his quick responses ("Clark's letters are nearly unique for their light shafts and needles of wit," wrote Dalton Camp), the next, emulating a caricature of former U.S. President Gerald Ford.

Inevitably, the Clark jokes and the collections of Clark gaffes began to accumulate in journalists' notebooks and prairie beer parlour conversations. It is tradition that public men are noted, at least during their years in public office, more for their fumbles and gaucheries than their brilliance. (Pierre Trudeau will always be recognized for his admonition to *"mange la merde"* and his mouthing in Parliament of "fuck-off," which finally reached Hansard as a bawdlerized "fuddle-duddle." Few recall his destruction of an opposition member with the off-hand comment, "The honourable member does not agree; I can hear his head shaking.") So also Joe Clark contributed mightily to the legend of his ham-fistedness with a skill amounting to genius for saying or doing the wrong thing while in range of camera or microphone.

Sometimes Maureen, regarded by many as the *really* tough member of the Clark family, was less than helpful. While junketing through Africa as part of his trip to the Commonwealth Conference in Lusaka, the new Prime Minister of Canada was invited to sign the V.I.P. guest book in the Moi Palace in Nairobi, Kenya. He signed his first name: "Joe." Then his pen ran dry; he had another but it carried red ink. "I don't want to sign my name in red," Clark muttered. But Maureen, oblivious, said audibly, "What have you done? Forgotten your name?" Clark signed his last name in red ink, the only red, white and blue signature in the book.

Outside the palace shortly after, posing with Kenya's government leaders for photos, the Canadian Prime Minister was standing beside his wife. "Well," announced Maureen, "this is enough of this standing around and smiling. Let's go and eat."

Probably the first (unrecorded) gaffe of Canada's new Prime Minister — if one discounts the Richard Nixon victory salute he gave to Alberta's Spruce Grove Arena and the nation's T.V. networks — came as the P.M.-elect left the arena. Alerted that Clark had won, the RCMP rushed extra security details to Spruce Grove to watch over the P.C. leader. As a result a huge, black limousine, complete with security-minded Mounties, was waiting for the victor when he left the arena after his victory speech. Unused to such luxury, Clark is reported to have climbed into the car and, unfamiliar with the spaciousness of such vehicles, promptly sat down on the floor, entirely missing the seat some inches behind his descending posterior.

Joe Clark knew that the public's perception of his personality was largely in the control of the press corps. The attitude of his government to the press was, however, not without contradictions. When emerging from the House or travelling, the Prime Minister was apparently fair game for radio and T.V. reporters; RCMP security guards, who had often moved soundmen away from Pierre Trudeau or brushed aside their intrusive boom microphones, took no such measures for Clark. All of this came about, one might speculate, because of the flying wedge of Ottawa police who escorted the new leader from his rostrum after he'd won the Tory leadership in 1976, irritating many P.C. delegates as well as Clark by insulating him from those who wished to press his flesh. But around the House of Commons, security became tighter; reporters and film crews were often asked to prove they'd been invited to interview this M.P., or that one; and some areas in the Centre Block that had previously been open to T.V. crews were declared off-limits for cameras.

Both Joe and Maureen proved themselves possessed of a degree of solicitude unknown in their predecessor. In the days of the Trudeau governments (and those of Pearson and Diefenbaker before him), cabinet meeting days could always be divined by the presence of reporters and T.V. film crews sitting on the floor in the corridor outside the cabinet sanctum, some engaged in conversation or desultory games of pitch-penny, some reading, some dozing away the time before the cabinet members would emerge. Joe Clark provided *chairs* in the hallway outside the cabinet room.

When Canada's provincial premiers met for dinner at 24 Sussex Drive, their last such gathering before the defeat of the 1979 Clark regime, reporters composed themselves for a long evening's wait on the front lawn; it wouldn't be the first such vigil spent awaiting that possible scoop or provocative comment as guests of the Prime Minister left after a good meal; often the journalistic watch had been kept in rain and snow. But not this time: Maureen McTeer had opened a room in the garage attached to the gatehouse, the home of the Prime Minister's chauffeur, and had despatched hot coffee in

china cups. The press corps was overwhelmed.

But Maureen, always her own woman, was also capable of being a very tough hostess. When Robert Stanfield, George Hees, and other Tory luminaries visited Stornoway, the official residence of the leader of the opposition after Joe Clark's election as party leader, the reception was different. Maureen interrupted their policy/strategy meeting to ask them to keep it down, because "the baby can't get to sleep."

It's easy to chart the spoor of Clark miscues, including those inflicted on him by inadequate staff. There was the

Calgary meeting during his leadership campaign, for example, during which he spoke in glowing terms of the virtues of small business, unaware he was addressing a gathering of multinational oil conglomerate executives. What's infinitely tougher for the political cartographer is getting a hard fix on Clark's philosophy and policies — even the pragmatic bench-marks of his craft and trade. In the early seventies, for example, Joe Clark clearly embraced the principle that capital punishment was a barbaric, mediaeval anethema; in the election campaign of 1979 the now Prime Minister made it clear, in Dalton Camp's contemptuous summary, that Canada could have "reinstitution of the death penalty, if only enough hangers could be elected to the next Parliament."

The man described by former M.P.-turned-columnist Douglas Fisher as "a tough and ruthless pragmatist" had learned in Camp's icy judgement that "Though a man must speak, he need not give offence by offering his own judgement." Clark, "the pliable man of infinite calculation and timidity," the man who "had developed a knack of apparent spontaneity," the fellow who would be "in a fight, the safest man around to hold your coat" — that man had won and lost the highest office of Canada in the space of seven months.

~ 3 ~

The Spearbearers: Murray and McTeer

"Canada celebrated the year of the child," said John Diefenbaker in the early summer of 1979, "by electing Joe Clark as Prime Minister." The Chief, disappointed both with Clark's leadership and with his campaign in the spring of 1979, had taken a sharp turn from his assessment during the convention of 1976. Then Diefenbaker had pronounced that Joe Clark "would make a remarkable leader of this party" and would "rejuvenate the House of Commons."

Even earlier — much earlier — in 1964, Clark had been drafted to introduce John Diefenbaker to a Progressive Conservative annual meeting made ugly by discontent with the Chief's leadership. Clark, who was, even in the view of his admiring biographer, "seeking to stay out of the quarrel as much as possible," made a masterful, short speech which stroked the wounded leader without betraying anything more than appropriate party loyalty. But Diefenbaker was deeply moved: "If there were no other rewards in public life than . . . what was stated by the brilliant Joe Clark I would have been rewarded more than I could have hoped for."

That was, of course, before Joe became leader. It was also before Joe Clark had employed Lowell Murray, a fellow who became Clark's chief advisor and strategist and who was, in the end, the chief architect of the destruction of the 1979 Clark government. As a member of Canada's Defence Forces, Lowell Murray could have been court-martialled. (Self-inflicted wounds, such as venereal disease, are serious matters in the army.) Instead, as a respected member of the P.C. legions, he was put in charge of Joe Clark's new election campaign, the campaign he had made inevitable.

Lowell Murray's career began as a T.V. reporter in Cape Breton, where he interviewed John Diefenbaker during the campaign of 1957. Murray next surfaced in Ottawa as executive assistant to Justice Minister Davie Fulton at the end of the fifties. When Fulton's wary support of a failed palace revolt against John Diefenbaker left the former Rhodes scholar persuaded there were greener pastures in the west, Lowell Murray went along. After surviving the whipping administered to Fulton as leader-without-a-party of the B.C. Conservatives, Murray reappeared in Ottawa, as aide to Senator Wallace McCutcheon. From that post he was loaned to assist in the Conservative general election campaign of 1965; it was Murray who spotted a slogan in Teddy White's *Making of a President, 1964* used by Nelson Rockefeller: "He Cares Enough To Come." Switched to "He Cared Enough To Come," it became the Tory byword in 1965, when John Diefenbaker visited 196 communities, mostly by train, while Lester Pearson jetted into only thirty-two. (Like Clark, Murray was a learner, but he took his cues from Pearson; in the 1979 campaign, Clark spent more time in airplanes than at rallies; exposures to voters were, above all, 'controlled.' He was never permitted to hazard gaffes in unprogrammed encounters.)

In 1966 Murray worked for the election of Dalton Camp

as national president of the Progressive Conservative Party. He manned a telephone in his boss, Wally McCutcheon's office to solicit nationwide support for the Camp candidacy and, by more than accidental implication, criticism of John Diefenbaker. But when McCutcheon ran for the P.C. leadership in 1967, Davie Fulton ran, too, and Murray went back to his prior loyalty. A hint of the sharp blade hidden behind Lowell Murray's shy smile: while campaigning in Quebec for Fulton, Murray heard a Duff Roblin supporter, Quebec P.C. President Paul Trepanier, telling reporters Roblin would get 300 of Quebec's 535 ballots at the convention. Murray, managing the Fulton campaign, countered by giving the press the names of three of the five delegates from Trepanier's own riding who were supporting *his* man.

After the fourth ballot at the P.C. convention, when Fulton was knocked out of the contest and moved to support Robert Stanfield, Murray and his associates scoured the lists of delegates for support for Stanfield. One of the campaign workers who moved onto the convention floor at Maple Leaf Gardens to sew up the Stanfield fifth ballot victory was Joe Clark, another Fulton worker. Clark, asked to join Stanfield's transitional Ottawa staff, persuaded the new leader to hire Lowell Murray as chief-of-staff for the opposition leader's office. The two young men shared an Ottawa apartment (with Graham Scott) at 80 Rideau Terrace, a trendy new address for members of the capital's swinging singles set. Murray was regarded as a superb ghost writer, one who often found occasion to rework Clark's speeches for Stanfield, to Joe's discomfiture.

By February of 1970 Murray, restless, had had enough; he moved to join the public relations department of the CNR. (Clark stayed only until May 1970, now elevated by default to the job of chief speech-writer for Bob Stanfield.) Murray went on to New Brunswick to be Premier Richard Hatfield's deputy minister and the second most powerful man in the province. Lowell Murray returned to Ottawa in 1976 with Hatfield to support Flora MacDonald's leadership candidacy; but within a year of the leadership campaign he was once again safely tucked up with his former pupil, Joe Clark, and in charge of building a campaign organization for 1979.

While Lowell Murray had been playing *eminence grise* in New Brunswick, Joe Clark had been building a parliamentary career. As Clark wrote in 1970,

> I realized that there were limits to what you can do in a staff job. A good staff member has to give advice to a leader that falls within the context of the initiatives of that leader. There were some things I wanted to do for myself . . . I wanted to be elected. I think my talents are greater in the front room. I have some in the back room but others are far more effective there than me.

Thus, it was decided that, in the football language of the thirties, Lowell Murray was to become "Mr. Inside," and Joe Clark "Mr. Outside." Now it was Murray who seemed more frequently present at meetings of both the inner and outer cabinet, and at the Prime Minister's side, than even Privy Council Clerk Marcel Masse, whom Murray had recommended as Clark's chief mandarin. Now it was the political pros, not the mandarin élite of a career civil service, as in the days of Pierre Trudeau's intimate dependence on Michael Pitfield, who had the Prime Minister's ear.

Lowell Murray's ubiquity is essential to a reading of the Clark government because Murray seemed, by late 1979, to be combination nanny, philosopher-king, and chief strategist. The role of tactician, disciplinarian (the guy who had to fire PMO staff who didn't measure up), and general factotum seemed to have fallen onto the ample lap of Bill Neville, a former executive assistant for Liberal Judy La Marsh and a brilliant, over-achieving work addict. Neville had proved his

Tory credentials by self-immolating in a race against John Turner in 1974, and been number one on the Clark team after 1976, following a tenure in the Tory federal research office and sundry chores for Bob Stanfield.

Before the Murray presence became all-encompassing, Maureen McTeer frequently played the nanny role, and as 1979 ended she may still have had as much policy heft as anyone. In the spring campaign of 1979, and through the early, heady days of high office (while Lowell Murray was fishing, again), Maureen was often seen to take the Prime Minister's elbow, tilting him toward the T.V. cameras or welcoming dignitaries. At other times the careful First Lady would slow her pace, holding Joe back, allowing film camera crews to get that essential ten-steps-ahead for the "walking shot" they needed for the late night news.

If Joe Clark ever felt the need for an infusion of "tough pills" they were, as no one doubted, readily available both from Murray and McTeer. Another brief note from the acid flask in which Dalton Camp dips his chrome-steel pen:

His wife . . . resolute smile and wary eyes. . . . Beneath that transparent sweetness there is iron enough, in the woman alone, for all the anvils in Canada. . . . Baodicea and Caesar would not have made a better pair for the strategies of conquest and the rule of pragmatism.

As for Murray:

The early blunders of Clark — the "stimulative deficit," and the apparent softness on separatism — were all committed while Murray had been tooling about Ireland. . . . Once he was back in town, and had the show on the road, the mistakes were few.

Not that there weren't a few. Not the least of which was the Tory campaign promise to move Canada's embassy in Israel from Tel Aviv to Jerusalem. But here Murray's advice was up against formidable counter-pressures from the other Big M in Joe Clark's life: Ms. McTeer. Even John Diefenbaker failed to dissuade the High River hustler from his plan to fish for Metro Toronto's Jewish votes with the glittering lure of a Zionist diplomatic coup.

On August 8, 1979, John Diefenbaker obtained a form of reinstatement and recognition from Canada's new Conservative Prime Minister. Banished to a cramped office by Mike Pearson after his electoral humiliation of 1963 and left to smother in his tiny quarters by Pearson's successor, Pierre Trudeau, John Diefenbaker was finally given an office suitable to his station and service just eight days before his death. Busy settling into his new, spacious Centre Block quarters in the middle of the Parliament Building's fourth floor, facing the expanse of lawns south of the Peace Tower, the Old Man received reporters in his new sanctum. He was less than fulsome in his gratitude to Prime Minister Clark as he yarned about the old days and indulged in his beloved penchant for political story-telling, satire, gossip, and mischief. Rumbled the Chief:

That young fellow [Clark] has only ever asked me for advice on one occasion. He phoned me, during the campaign, to say he was thinking of promising to move our embassy to Jerusalem. The course I recommended was that he forget it. It could only cause trouble, I said. And the next day — the very next day — that young man went out and did the very opposite to the course I had recommended to him. That's the history of our relationship.

John Diefenbaker's absolute veracity was sometimes as

© Yardley Jones/Canada-Wide

frail as his commitment to discretion; but if his recital was accurate, he had for once given excellent advice to a man holding the office he had always believed should be his own.

Joe Clark, though, had been given other advice. Ron Atkey, who'd lost Toronto's St. Paul's seat to Liberal Secretary of State John Roberts in 1974 by just 1,129 votes, still hungered and hankered for the riding; and the riding had a substantial Jewish vote. And Ron Atkey, who had never stopped running in the 1974/1979 interregnum, had a friend named Jeff Lyons; and Jeff Lyons had tutored, of all people, Maureen McTeer, when she was cramming for some law exams.

So Ron Atkey, who'd been spoken to by several constituents of the Jewish faith and of Zionist persuasion, spoke to
his good friend Jeff Lyons, who spoke to his pupil and scholas-
tic debtor, Maureen McTeer, who spoke to her child's father,
Joe. Soon after, Joe took the first long step toward the lethal
"flip-flop" image that was to bedevil him in the heat of August
and destroy him in cruel December. Like a DNA molecule or a
human cell, programming itself for death after a preordained
period, Joe Clark had begun to move his still-unelected
government toward defeat before it left the electoral womb.

~ 4 ~

The Embassy Move:
A Metaphor of Method

For the vast majority of Canadian voters, the question of where Canada's embassy in Israel was to be located was one of, at best, minor significance in the 1979 election campaign. Even in those days of energy scares, most Canadians probably would not, for example, have begrudged our consular officials the extra gasoline they'd have needed to commute from Jerusalem to Tel Aviv (to meet with Israeli government officials who are mostly housed there).

Nor, despite the resident paranoia of some Tory cabinet ministers and advisors, did the Canadian media take undue advantage of the Jerusalem gaffe. In fact, the Jerusalem promise triggered a stunning example of journalistic probity and responsibility. Not one commentator, for example, suggested that in the event of such a move, and given the hostility of the Palestine Liberation Organization to such an action, our Canadian peace-keeping troops serving with the United Nations in the Middle East would become instant and obvious targets for PLO reprisal. More than one reporter, this one among them, considered the virtually defenceless condition of our troops around Israel; not one journalist risked generating PLO attacks on them by mentioning their vulnerability in print, on radio or on T.V.

But the Jerusalem promise did have general and overpowering consequences: it sustained cynics in their contempt of politicians, and more than other Clark policies, it encouraged voters, opposition parties, and reporters to see in the 1979 Clark government an expedient philosophy geared only to short-term electoral results, *sans* principle or conviction.

Of the approximately 51,000 voters in St. Paul's riding in 1979, all three major parties agreed, about 23 per cent were Jewish, and Canadian elections often swing on the hinge offered by a 5-per-cent switch in votes.

In 1972, Ron Atkey, then a thirty-year-old Toronto lawyer, had squeaked by the Liberals to win the coveted Metro Toronto seat by 828 votes. Atkey wanted the seat back after his narrow defeat in 1974. Ironies breed with such enthusiasm in politics that most are scarcely worth noting, but one commands attention here. In 1976, when Flora MacDonald was seeking the leadership of the P.C. Party of Canada, her assistant campaign manager was that well-known and well-connected Toronto Red Tory, Ron Atkey. Three brief years later the Atkey-inspired embassy pledge was making Flora's first days in External Affairs an agony of embarrassments. While Flora struggled to endorse publicly a policy she knew to be witless, possibly dangerous, Atkey and Clark ably assisted her inquisitors from the press in inflicting a daily death-of-a-thousand-unkind-cuts on the bloody but loyal Secretary of State for External Affairs. Rarely had the doctrine of cabinet solidarity been more sorely tested.

Ron Atkey aside, Clark's campaign aides advised against the promise. When they met in Ottawa in mid-April, it had been agreed such a policy was too risky, politically. But

Toronto was the Big Apple in the 1979 campaign, filled with creamy seats ripe for the taking from a faltering Liberal grasp; and St. Paul's had been a "close one" in 1974. So Joe Clark called Ottawa from his Toronto hotel room to report the pressure on him to make the promise. Lowell Murray was on the Ottawa end of the phone, and he didn't even like the question. "Use your own judgement," Murray had been reported to say. Clark did.

Joe Clark's agreement to the embassy move idea in April was no shock to those who knew him well, although it represented a 180-degree turn from his first public statement on the issue. Clark, always an ardent supporter of Israel, had been wooing Jewish voters and financial support since the summer of 1977. But he'd held off any comment on the issue until January of 1979. Then, in Israel after being arm twisted by Israeli Premier Menacham Begin to support such a policy, Clark said a polite no. It would, said the opposition leader in a Jerusalem press conference, "be inappropriate at this time for Canada to make any move that would be interpreted in a way that would divert attention of all parties from the pursuit of the Camp David accords."

Two months later, on March 22, the election in Canada was called, just four days before Premier Begin and Anwar Sadat signed their peace treaty at the White House. By late April Clark was under heavy pressure from both Atkey and Rob Parker, the Conservative candidate in another heavily Jewish riding in Toronto, Eglinton. (Both had accompanied the leader on his January visit to Israel and had subsequently larded their campaign literature with pictures of themselves in the Jewish state.) When Clark announced his embassy policy on April 25 (to the horror of External Affairs experts, who'd dissuaded Pierre Trudeau from the same course in November 1978), it was just minutes before he met with the Toronto representatives of the Canada–Israel committee.

Jerusalem is, beyond doubt, a holy city to the world's

Jews, as it is to the world's Christians, and the world's Moslems. Indeed, in one of those minor paradoxes of history, Solomon had built his temple in Jerusalem on the site of what was later to become a Moslem place of worship: the modern Wailing Wall of Jerusalem is actually a retaining wall of that Moslem architecture.

When the Israelis conquered all of Jerusalem in the 1967 war, there were thirteen embassies and consulates located in the Jewish (Western) quarter of the city. But only one country of considerable stature, the Netherlands was there. Israel, of course, had precisely the same legal right to eastern Jerusalem as Jordan had had in the years from 1948 to 1967. That is, like Jordan, Israel had taken the rest of the city by force of arms, but their victory did not draw any new embassies to the Holy City.

There were, however, other politicians who considered the vote-getting advantages of such a move. In 1976, while Ron Atkey was beating the bushes for Flora MacDonald's leadership campaign, a U.S. Democrat from Georgia was in search of the presidential nomination — and the U.S. Jewish votes that could help him in the moneyed, northeastern states. So Jimmy Carter, three years before Joe Clark, promised, if nominated and elected, to move the U.S. embassy from Tel Aviv to Jerusalem. Once elected, however, Carter allowed the pledge to quietly slip to the back burner. The times weren't propitious for controversial actions by the peanut farmer with his eye on a global image.

The question getting the most attention on Ottawa's diplomatic row on Monday, June 4, 1979, as Joe Clark was sworn into office as Prime Minister, the sixteenth man to take that oath, was whether he meant it, whether he'd follow Carter's example or feel obliged to follow through on the party platform.

The diplomats were not kept in suspense for long. Minutes after she was sworn as Canada's Minister of External

Affairs, Flora MacDonald bit down through a strained smile and told reporters the embassy "will be moved . . . as Mr. Clark has indicated," and, a small loophole here, "in a period of time that is containable." The following day, on his fortieth birthday, Canada's shiny new and more-assured Prime Minister hammered home the message. Clad in a new, cream-coloured suit (the day before, the trousers, too long by several inches, had caught under his shoes at a Tory caucus; today the suit was appropriately cuffed) the smiling P.M. brushed aside press suggestions the move might be forgotten, or re-thought. "Those questions are now beyond discussion as to their appropriateness," said the Prime Minister, carefully and deliberately. "We certainly intend to do that. . . . What we will be seeking from the Public Service will be indications as to how we accomplish what we have undertaken to do. I can't give you a timetable at this stage." There was to be "no slackening in the commitment. Period. Or, at least, semi-colon.

As a self-acknowledged quick learner, Clark should have remembered the furious Arab response to an early speech in which he rhapsodized on the Jewish state shortly after he became P.C. leader in 1976. That reaction was nothing compared to that which was en route in 1979.

Response to Clark's reiterated and unequivocal intention to proceed on June 5 was swift. Just one day later ambassadors from Arab League countries in Canada demanded a meeting with Flora MacDonald. She refused to contradict the Prime Minister, but did offer a tiny placebo. Canada would not act, she said, "without deliberation."

That same day, June 6, 1979, the PLO called Clark's plan "an act of aggression" in a furious press release; and Canada's Arab lobby, the Canada–Arab Federation, described the move as "a declaration of war on 900 million Moslems." Said a spokesman for Yassir Arafat ominously: "The Palestinians know how to deal with this dangerous matter in a way that will safeguard their rights."

And, still on June 6, the federal civil service began a war of attrition with the brand new government. The bureaucrats saw as their first duty the need to preserve and protect basic Canadian policies and Canada's role in the world. In the next few weeks many Conservatives in the new government were to see the Ottawa public service as protectors, chiefly, of old Liberal policies. But the mandarins served Flora MacDonald well in her need to preserve a façade of cabinet unity while delaying a fatal foreign policy initiative. Said unnamed spokesmen in External Affairs on June 6: "Arab states might welcome the embassy move as it would permit them [the Arabs] to make an example of Canada via economic and terrorist reprisal." Another spokesman in the federal department of Trade and Commerce stated that "Canada exported $885-million worth of merchandise to Middle Eastern Arab countries last year; and besides the possibility of losing that trade," he added, "you can throw in another half-billion dollars in consulting services we are exporting."

In Washington on June 6, a spokesman for the U.S. State Department, unsettled by the Clark press conference, reported ominously that "the views of the American government have been made clear to the Clark government" — a government now less than two days in office.

On Friday, June 8, Ron Atkey denied the issue had been a key factor in his election May 22; but he vowed to carry through on the move: "That's what I was elected to do, and I will."

The fact Clark's Catch-22 was of his own devising made it no easier to bear. If the Prime Minister held firm, he courted a stunning array of economic (and potential terrorist) reprisals; if he changed the stated policy of his government he'd be seen as a vacillating leader. Virtually every observer, the week of June 4, had sensed a new poise and assurance in the P.C. leader. The growing confidence he'd shown in flashes through the April/May campaign seemed to have hardened into a genuine and fixed sense of comfort and destiny. At a birthday party given him by the neophyte Prime Minister's Office staff in the Langevin Block, June 5, Joe had ceremoniously cut the first slice of the cake; then, as he prepared to continue, Maureen had whispered that he should get someone else to complete the job. There were several versions of Joe's next remark, as his back stiffened perceptibly and his smile became a shade fixed. But a sound tape made at the time gives the verbatim quote: The Prime Minister turned to his wife, the take-charge lady through much of his campaign, and muttered, "I assume any fool could cut a cake, Maureen."

Clark did not, anymore, see himself as a bumbler; and he was making it clear to all those around him that his tolerance threshold for any aspersions to his social or political skills was very low.

The Prime Minister's "flip-flop" image went back to the days shortly after his election as party leader, when he'd felt required to abort a hugely embarrassing battle for the P.C. federal nomination in the riding of Bow River, in Alberta. Under redistribution, Joe Clark's old riding of Rocky Mountain had been split, and his hometown of High River was now in the new Bow River constituency. The adjacent new riding, Yellowhead, also had a large chunk of Clark's former voters in it, but the P.C. leader opted to run in Bow River, despite the previous announcement by the sitting (Conservative) M.P. for the old Palliser Riding that he, Stan Schumacher, intended to run in Bow River. Their public wrangling over the Tory nomination was mercifully brief but deeply humiliating to Clark, who finally took the excellent advice of his campaign staff and agreed to run in Yellowhead. No one could calculate the damage to his self-esteem, but the public wound was considerable. In the words of his biographer: "Bow River was interpreted by some as a sign of weakness in Clark at the very time that many Canadians were asking whether he was tough enough for leadership. First he staked out untenable ground. Then he failed to defend it."

Described by one acute observer as a man of surprisingly small ego for a politician but of considerable vanity, the new Prime Minister was in no rush to become the victim of an international Bow River incident. And there were other times in his past the young P.M. felt he had to live down. Although he'd gained an M.A. in political science for his thesis on innovation in political conventions, he had failed to complete his law studies. Although few journalists mentioned that master's thesis, many waspishly reminded the public that Clark was a drop-out from the professional discipline being studied by Maureen. (Less than three months after becoming leader, Clark had achieved a piece of his earlier goal when he was awarded an honourary Doctorate of Laws at the University of New Brunswick. Interestingly, given the tight political/ social/economic and academic linkages in the Maritimes, and especially in New Brunswick, Joe's honourary degree was bestowed, May 13, 1976, just three months before Lowell Murray, his previous mentor and next-year strategist, left the Fredericton corridors of power for a year at Queen's University.)

The context and the lesson were clear: the law school and Bow River drop-out didn't want to get caught doing that again, ever again.

The heat under the embassy pressure cooker was seemingly turned up a notch every day of the Clark administration's first week in office, despite Flora MacDonald's best efforts to cool out the crisis. On Thursday, June 7, Flora told reporters there would be no initiatives to move the embassy before Parliament met in the autumn, probably in October. But by Friday some Arab newspapers were publishing threats of an oil boycott against Canada; on Saturday, June 9, the governments of Saudi Arabia and several gulf oil states were quoted in Beirut as adding the threat of a boycott of Canadian companies with fat contracts in the Middle East.

That same day, Saturday, Miss MacDonald said she was

"not aware of any warnings received from the Arab states by the Canadian government," but she had another olive branch: "We are prepared to make accommodations with the Arab states over this move and we will be discussing with them how best we can carry out our stated intentions." Moreover, the government "will attach a very high priority to determine (sic) its impact on our role as a peace-keeping nation in the area."

But there was domestic political pressure, too, from Jewish community leaders in Canada to press ahead. So Flora had something for them, as well, and a denial of any waffling: "The embassy *will be moved. There should be no doubt about that.*"

Perhaps as embarrassing to the Minister of External Affairs as the unremitting questions of reporters trying unsuccessfully to force her to confess a personal distaste for the policy were the opinions of her new international colleagues. Just a week after being sworn into office she was to leave for meetings of the OECD (Economic Cooperation and Development) nations in Paris; two weeks later there was the Western nations' economic summit meeting in Tokyo, and the first week in August, there would be the gathering of Commonwealth heads of state at Lusaka, Zambia. Few held grand hopes for Canada's prestige among other international leaders while the government was struggling to free itself from a thicket of brambles into which it had leapt, voluntarily, to secure two marginal Toronto seats. And many of the African Commonwealth leaders with whom Clark and Mac-Donald would have to parley at Lusaka were openly pro-Arab in policy.

More pressure and more reassurances were to come. By the end of the week of June 4, Menachem Begin had personally telephoned Joe Clark to thank him for sticking to his pledge — surely not the most welcome call of the week. Statistics Canada weighed in on the side of status quo, reaffirming that Canadian trade to the Middle East had totalled $85 million in the single month of March 1979. Trade

Minister Bob de Cotret, a rising cabinet star (though a defeated candidate, he was about to be appointed to the Senate) promised that "trade is one of . . . the considerations that have to be examined before acting."

Even Joe Clark had found a new caveat. On Monday, June 11, in an interview on U.S. television, Clark said he'd like to have a "written guarantee of free access to all the sites in Jerusalem which are sacred to Christians, Jews, and Moslems" before proceeding.

In an interview published in *The Globe and Mail* June 13, and written by Clark biographer David Humphreys, Flora MacDonald said the embassy move had been discussed by the P.C. caucus, but not in cabinet. Miss MacDonald denied that U.S. Ambassador Thomas Enders had put any pressure on the Clark government to change the policy, but with her usual candor she added that he did mention it casually in a congratulatory phone call.

Now the columnists began to tote up the possible cost to Canada of Arab reaction: Bell Telephone had huge contracts in the Middle East; Air Canada had just signed a contract to service Saudi Arabia's fleet of L-1011 aircraft; on the same day Miss MacDonald's interview was published, Westinghouse Canada announced its fears it might lose an $85-million contract in Libya — this in a front-page story noting that Bell's Saudi Arabian deal for $1.5 billion was also in jeopardy.

There was more to come. On June 19, the Arab Monetary Fund formally announced in Bahrain it would make no further deposits with Canadian banks. Our dollar promptly dropped from $.8525 (U.S.) to $.8490. (In Paris, Flora MacDonald had been heard with more than perfunctory sympathy when, speaking in support of foreign aid, she commented, "It's often difficult to see the long-term advantages instead of the immediate problems.")

By June 16, a team of *Toronto Star* reporters, working with figures supplied by the Canadian Export Association, had calculated Canadians would lose anywhere from 23,000 to 67,500 jobs if Arab threats to boycott Canadian goods were made good. Two days later the Canadian Council of Churches waded into the fray with a message to the Prime Minister that the embassy move "would advance neither peace nor justice nor reconciliation in the Middle East."

The same day the Arab Monetary Fund announcement was pummelling the Canadian dollar, Ron Atkey, now elevated to cabinet rank with the twin portfolios of Immigration and Employment, misjudged his aim and poured oil on the fire instead of coating the troubled political waters. Under attack as the man responsible for unemployment abatement in Canada, Atkey questioned Arab willingness to back their boycott threats. Besides, added the man who'd pushed Joe Clark into the policy, the Arab's "bark is worse than their bite."

This time the barks followed immediately. Yassir Arafat made his own statement in Kuwait: "Our Arab nation must teach the Canadian scoundrels a lesson that would ensure the protection of our dignity." A group of ten Arab state ambassadors in Ottawa issued a formal statement charging that the Immigration Minister's slight was "a profound infringement on Arab dignity and honour." In Jordan, a government-backed newspaper said the Arab states would consider closing their Ottawa embassies. The Arab ambassadors told an embarrassed Minister of External Affairs the Atkey miscue was "a shattering blow to the prevailing friendship between the Canadian and the Arab peoples."

In the Langevin Block the Prime Minister's staff, well aware there were far more grave threats to Canada's economy and much deeper political and social problems on the horizon, agonized over one face-saving formula after another. They had a deadline: the diplomatic python strangling their credibility had to be scotched before Parliament assembled on October 9. Bad enough that this government was waiting longer after its election to meet the House of Commons than

any other government in Canada's history; there was also
Question Period to be considered, and that ubiquitous elec-
tronic eye, capable of carrying the government's daily discomfiture into homes across the land.

On June 22, Joe Clark met with representatives of his
party's historic allies, a delegation of ten national business
leaders which included Canadian Manufacturers' Association
president, John Bulman. The Prime Minister indicated, said
Bulman, that he would "try to reduce the impact" of which
the businessmen warned him.

Then on June 23, the Prime Minister permitted Arab
diplomats to by-pass normal practice and, in a series of "extraordinary meetings," talked in turn with nine Arab League
ambassadors, as well as with the representatives of Egypt and
Israel in separate meetings. Reasonably well-informed Ottawa
gossip, probably fueled by "test leaks" from the PMO, had it
that the P.M. was considering despatching a "goodwill
mission" to the Arab states; additionally, just as Jordan was
about to urge Arab states to shut down their Ottawa embassies
and consulates, the PMO announced the possibility that an
embassy might be opened in Jordan — Canada's first there.
Canada might also, as a gesture to placate Premier Begin (and
those voters in St. Paul's and Eglinton), open a small consular
office, or maybe an immigration office, in Jerusalem. (Mr.
Atkey could have the honour of opening an immigration
office, as it fell under his authority; some of his caucus
colleagues also suggested he be seconded to it, as a permanent
staff of one.)

The meetings with the Arab diplomats came, literally, on
the eve of Joe Clark's departure for the Tokyo summit meetings. The new boy in the Langevin Block was determined not
to arrive at table with Jimmy Carter, Margaret Thatcher, and
the rest, without first having wiped the embassy egg from his
political countenance. But the placebos offered up by the
P.M.'s strategists clearly weren't going to be good enough.

© 1979. Reprinted with permission of the *Toronto Star* Syndicate.

Those who claim to know say the ultimate compromise came from the chief public victim of the embassy policy, Flora MacDonald. Certainly it reflected her mastery of political craft; and it probably required her considerable powers of persuasion with her old and good friend, a man from whom she could call the I.O.U.'s gathered during many tough campaigns on which she worked as a party worker and organizer. Robert Stanfield, the man who'd been succeeded by Joe Clark, has a deep-rooted, almost Calvinist loyalty to his party, but he badly wanted rest and peace. It's unlikely anyone but his beloved Flora could have recruited him as the embassy-move fireman.

Clark met the Arab ambassadors at 24 Sussex Drive on the morning of Saturday, June 23; in the afternoon he went on to talk with Egyptian representative Fahmy. But he was unable to meet with Israel's ambassador, Mordechai Shalev, until 9:30 P.M., after the summer sunset signalled the end of the Jewish Sabbath. The final (and probably toughest) meeting over, Joe Clark met reporters at the front door of his official residence, the darkness vanquished by portable T.V. lights. The weary Prime Minister read a statement obviously prepared the evening before. Former P.C. Leader Robert Stanfield had agreed, said Clark, to act as the P.M.'s "special representative" in an effort to work out a solution to the thorny problem.

Never, apparently, a man to accept survival gracefully, Clark told the press representatives standing in the penumbra of the T.V. lights that he was "still committed" to moving the embassy. But, flinching only a trifle, he hastily added that he would, of course, await Stanfield's recommendations, which he did not expect, "until next year." After all, with that Tokyo plane due to leave in less than twelve hours, and Parliament to face in October, it would be as well to get the issue as far from public scrutiny as possible, for as long as possible.

"I wouldn't want to confine Mr. Stanfield to an exact timetable," said the Prime Minister. "I want to see the implementation of our policy on Jerusalem in a way that will be compatible with the efforts that are being made to achieve a comprehensive peace settlement in the Middle East."

By the time the P.M.'s office issued the formal statement, there was no mention of Joe Clark's being "still committed" to the move. Flora MacDonald, who unlike John Diefenbaker and Lowell Murray had first heard of Joe Clark's Jerusalem policy from the press, back in the halcyon days of April, was, probably through her own wit and intelligence, off the hook.

Of course a spokesman in the PMO still had a little kerosene left to toss on the dying embers: any suggestion that Bob Stanfield might actually oppose the move after his study was "purely hypothetical," a reporter was told.

Thirty-six hours later, still exuding relief, Joe Clark told U.S. President Jimmy Carter, who'd said the Canadian P.M. looked well: "Well, I feel pretty well. I guess winning helps. It perks you up."

Talking with *Toronto Star* columnist Richard Gwyn on the flight home from Tokyo later, Clark had forgotten all the staff conferences at which, in March, the embassy move policy had been vetoed. "I had not had a chance to be briefed on all the nuances," explained the Prime Minister. So he had "moved too early."

In the same interview, Clark described the damage done to him as "a scar that will always be there, although not too large." Not a lyrical description, but candid. The scar may not, in Clark's opinion, have been too large, but it did join law school, Bow River, and the other itchy lumps chasing his psyche. And in the end they proved embarrassing enough that the Prime Minister, wanting to avoid additional humiliations, was blind to the parliamentary dangers lurking in December.

Now it remained to be certain the opposition had no real opportunity to rub the government's nose in the spoor of the issue. Privy Council President Walter Baker announced in late July that the Clark team would withhold planned legislation to prevent Canadian companies complying with Arab demands that no Israelis or Jews be employed on Arab contracts. The promised legislation might "short-circuit" Bob Stanfield's study, said Baker.

Stanfield himself, probably still choking on the elephantine bullet he'd been persuaded to bite for the good of the party, had nothing to say, at all. On September 9 the former Tory leader lifted off on a round of Middle Eastern talks. On the 13th he admitted to reporters in Jerusalem that "my terms of reference are very broad." He added that his survey of possibilities would be completed with a view to Canada's potential role as peace-keeper. "It's in this context, of course, that I'll be considering the embassy question."

Stanfield had nothing to add to that elliptical hint. Israeli reporters trying to find Canada's ambassador-at-large, as he'd been dubbed at home, began referring to him instead as "the phantom envoy." The Canadian embassy in Tel Aviv, helping the rangy Stanfield keep a low profile, said he must be treated as "a private visitor" to Israel.

While Bob Stanfield was leaving Israel for visits to Turkey, Jordan, Saudi Arabia, Iraq, Syria, and Lebanon, staff in the PMO were telling reporters the former Nova Scotia premier had been given "until the autumn of 1980" to complete his report. In that respect Bob Stanfield was to prove a deep disappointment to Joe Clark, bringing in a study that could only embarrass the Prime Minister before the minority government had been given even a month to settle into the House of Commons.

On October 16, a week after Parliament finally met, Michael Wilson, Minister of State for International Trade, surprised critics of the embassy policy by volunteering hard figures on business lost in Canada by the putative move. The forty-one-year-old former cub scout leader said, "There aren't any good effects from the move. . . . There's no doubt it's causing Canadian companies difficulty in doing business in the Middle East." Specifically, said Wilson, three "signed contracts with Arab countries" had been lost, with a price tag of $4.5 million to the Canadian firms involved. Other business in the area, he added, was "below normal."

Wilson's frank statement to the House of Commons wasn't made entirely gratuitously. A few days earlier, on October 12, he'd told an opposition questioner there had been no contracts lost by the government policy. On the Monday, October 15, he told the House he'd been mistaken. He had in fact been given a departmental memo on the matter back in June, as he conceded later, but "hadn't read the memo because of the pressures of new government." Opposition members suggested privately that they had read the memo, leaked to them by civil servants still waging their battle against the move. It was the certain knowledge that the opposition would reveal the document, and its date, that prompted the display of ministerial candour, they suggested. Or, in the memorable words of Dr. Sam Johnson, "Nothing concentrates a man's mind so wonderfully as the knowledge he is about to be hanged."

Three days later Bob Stanfield, now back in Ottawa, told reporters he'd have to travel some more, probably in November, before completing his report to the Prime Minister in 1980. That same day, October 19, Clark made it clear he was in no hurry: "I do not have any intention to meet with him [Stanfield] at present, or seek a preliminary report," said the P.M. But he was wrong, again; it was time for Prime Minister Clark to bite *his* bullet.

Stanfield met with Joe Clark on Friday, October 26, and told the P.M. that he wanted to submit an "interim report" right away. The Arab states were so preoccupied over the embassy question, said Stanfield, they refused to discuss any other matters until it was settled. Further delay might save early embarrassment in Parliament, but it could only exacerbate the continuing economic and diplomatic pain inflicted on Ottawa. Clark accepted the advice; and, true to his often stated principles of conducting a more open government, having agreed to expose his "scar" to the House and the public, he courageously agreed, too, to release the full text of a Stanfield report he knew could only diminish his own image.

On the Monday, October 29, Joe Clark told the House of Commons, for his government, that "we do not intend to move the embassy from Tel Aviv to Jerusalem."

At least, that's what the Prime Minister finally said,

having first waffled just a little in a formally prepared statement to the effect that "the government accepts the recommendation that no action be taken on the location of the
Canadian embassy until the status of Jerusalem is clarified
within a comprehensive agreement between Israel and its
Arab neighbours."

Having tabled the Stanfield interim report and taken his
medicine, the Prime Minister had to bite down during scath-
ing reactions from opposition leader Pierre Trudeau and New
Democratic Party leader Ed Broadbent. Pressed by Trudeau
to explain whether the embassy policy actually had "been
changed or is it merely the implementation of it which has
been delayed?" the Prime Minister tried to fudge the issue
one more time: "Mr. Speaker, it is not now our intention to
move the Canadian embassy in Israel to Jerusalem."

Pierre Trudeau responded: "Mr. Speaker, I think the
word 'now' is very, very crucial. . . . These are the words he
used; I ask the Prime Minister to clarify them."

Now Joe Clark was well and truly impaled by the blade he
himself had fashioned in a suite at Toronto's Prince Hotel
back on April 25. He replied, "Excuse me, Mr. Speaker, what I
should have said is 'it is not now our policy.' We do not intend
to move the embassy from Tel Aviv to Jerusalem. If there is a
just and lasting peace settlement that settles and clarifies the
question of Jerusalem, that may allow us to reopen the question. Until there is such a clarification within the context of a
just and lasting peace settlement, the Canadian embassy will
stay in Tel Aviv."

The House moved on to introduce a bill designed to
provide for the preservation of constituency documents
collected by M.P.s. The door had been left open by the width
of a hair, but the crack was too small to permit any slight ray
of sunshine for Menachem Begin and the voters of St. Paul's
and Eglinton, who now felt themselves betrayed as well as
manipulated.

Bob Stanfield's interim report, eagerly scrambled for by members of the press gallery, poured salt into the wound. It offered no apology for the original policy, suggested no rational motive for it, nor any merit in it:

> We must retain credibility with both sides as . . . fair-minded. . . . We could not do this if we were to move our embassy to Jerusalem. The transfer of the Canadian embassy in Israel from Tel Aviv to Jerusalem would be viewed by the Arabs as . . . prejudging the outcome of negotiations which have not yet taken place.

Nor was the PMO placebo, some "other" consular office for Jerusalem, an attractive notion:

> I do not recommend a consular office be established in Jerusalem. There is little practical need for such an office for consular purposes.

Joe Clark, as soon as he'd answered the Trudeau questions, left the House to its business. He refused to speak to the reporters waiting in the lobby. The scar was throbbing enough. Flora MacDonald and Ron Atkey answered a couple of questions each in the members' lobby, then returned to the sanctuary of the House.

Rabbi J. Benjamin Friedberg had his letter to the Prime Minister published in the *Toronto Star* a week later. The black headline over it, running across half the page, read: "Mr. Clark, I feel I've been had." The illustration in the body of the text showed a boyish Joe Clark reviewing Canadian peace-keeping troops on the Golan Heights the previous January. The shot had been taken during a day in which the future Prime Minister reportedly almost impaled himself on a Canadian bayonet as he rounded a rank of soldiers, a weapon a good deal less lethal, in the event, than a Tory platform plank.

Then in early November the government revealed that the Stanfield interim report, which had essentially remade the same points made by Joe Clark in the Middle East the previous January, had cost Canadian taxpayers $350,000.

As noted earlier, the Jerusalem morass was far from being the issue most central to Canadians at large, either during the campaign of April and May or the long weeks until the interim report. But throughout the period, Canadians had been mesmerized by the spectacle of a Prime Minister who seemed, despite an evidently faulty balance mechanism in his middle ear, determined to venture again and again onto the high wire stretched above a cage of man-eating tigers. Some admiration had been felt in the audience; but more suffered the self-conscious embarrassment of concert-goers listening to a young tenor who can't quite manage the C above high C, but is too proud to stop trying. (Mixed policies, one concedes, are often father to similar metaphors.)

Every government develops an image, a shorthand metaphor by which the public can easily describe its reaction to a leader. Usually such labels and logos fail to achieve general acceptance until after the new leader's honeymoon period is over. Often they are cruel, and as often perhaps unfair. But, like the "temper of the house," they are fundamental and inescapable barometers of political climate. So, as Pierre Trudeau had moved from admiration ("the mocking swinger") to pity ("weary and hag-ridden"), Joe Clark had moved from enigma ("Joe Who?") to ridicule ("The turkey").

Evidence both of his political savvy and his very considerable courage came with Clark's capacity, even in the dark days of October and December, to laugh at himself, even to retail his latest gaffes to members of the press corps. But the scar was no longer "not too large," and there was evidence it might fester.

Interregnum

We have looked at the mechanics and tactics that brought about the destruction of the 1979 Clark government on December 13, 1979. We have had a chance to examine what experiences and motives may have propelled Joe Clark toward his Parliament Hill crucifixion, and to consider which of his advisors contributed to the development of the hard-line stance that left the Clark front benches in the House able only to shatter rather than bend in that cathedral of compromise. Finally, there has been a review of the Jerusalem embassy affair, that classic metaphor for the method and the madness in Ottawa between April and December 1979.

But prime ministers walk a stage much wider than that encompassed by the members' lobbies and the strategy plotting rooms of the Hill's Centre Block. Every Canadian prime minister has a series of constituencies far beyond that from which he was elected. There are the worlds of international affairs, of federal-provincial relations, of Parliament, of the voters at large to consider; and, closer to home in the early days in office, the hothouse world of Ottawa itself.

It is first to that peculiar, closed society, the incestuous castes of Ottawa, that every government must attend. Each new prime minister must seek to penetrate the defences and achieve the support of the inhabitants of those myriad, nesting boxes that make up the Ottawa power generators. The diplomats, the bureaucratic mandarins, the military brass, the lobbyists, journalists, hostesses, restauranteurs, security staff, and technocrats, the syncophants, hangers-on, wishers-after, and those fearful of their jobs and their futures: all of them are inclined by nature and conditioning to turn inward, toward their peers, for security, support reassurance; few of them are anxious for new initiatives, new policies, new bosses. Like Parliament itself, which is the source of their power and their reason for being (though they seldom remember that), they want to be wooed not won. They regard themselves, not as the spoils of political wars, but rather as the civilizing influence needed to bring the raw, young barbarians through a necessary transition from freebooter to staid merchantman.

When they use the power they have fought countless silent, memo-wars to accumulate, it is information that fuses their heaviest artillery; they are reluctant to part with any of that precious armament. It's knowledge that best serves their ambition and protects their individual fiefdoms, and it's to be shared only with a miser's caution, or a virgin's anxiety. But it is, first and always, to the Ottawa constituency that each government must go, for nourishment after the battle, and for the intelligence needed to survive until the bugles blow again.

~ 5 ~

Ottawa: Life in the Hothouse

Joe Clark deliberately stayed away from Ottawa for the first few days after his election. He went instead to the CNR's Jasper Park Lodge, where he rested, met with advisors, planned his first days in office, and received briefings from the Liberal Privy Council Clerk Michael Pitfield, whom he summoned from Ottawa. Pitfield arrived with a trunk-load of bulging attache cases containing the instruments and advisories required for the transference of power. Pitfield, a Trudeau appointee and close friend of the former Prime Minister, wore his mandarin suit to the Jasper meeting. He was greeted by an orlon-sweatered, putative Prime Minister and looked out of place and out of context to a gratifying degree. (He was soon, too, to be out-of-work. In the course of their conversations, Clark told Pitfield he would want his resignation. Pitfield held his tongue, and Clark saved announcement of his first mandarin execution until his first Ottawa press conference, as Prime Minister, June 5.)

On Sunday, May 27, five days after the election, the Prime Minister-elect boarded an Air Canada flight from Edmonton to Ottawa. Never unable to pass up an opportunity for a little harmless (if pious) image-building, Clark refused the offer of a government JetStar: "I want to keep in touch with the problems Canadians face," he said — surely no compliment to Air Canada. "We don't [want] to become an aloof government." Not that it was quite a case of "just us folks" on the People's Airline. The Clarks rode first class (although RCMP security guard Guy Sauvé was relegated to economy). Federal health inspectors also took time to examine and analyze the food and water loaded aboard the Lockheed 1011, perhaps causing the delay that brought the flight into Ottawa five minutes late.

With eight days before he would be sworn to office Joe Clark had a busy but, in his own description, lonely schedule. The isolation of power was already settling about him; he later told a reporter he dropped in on former opposition leader Robert Stanfield several times to find "the only person I could talk to" and to have an audience for his musings about the cabinet he had to select and name within a week.

Already one decision made at the first Jasper retreat had been discarded. At Jasper it had been agreed the first Clark cabinet could include well over thirty members, with a high-powered twelve-member "inner cabinet." After a sobering day or two in Ottawa it was agreed the Clark government would have trouble building an image of restraint with so large a group — the cabinet would only have twenty-nine members, with eight elevated to special, inner-cabinet status.

Clark went further in efforts to make his new government match his determination to go on driving his blue Chev in place of the $84,000, silver-grey, armoured limousine ordered for Pierre Trudeau by security forces. New cabinet ministers, he announced, would not be provided with the services of fellow Tory M.P.s as parliamentary secretaries.

These caucus aides, available to answer questions in the House during the absence of their minister, and otherwise act as back-ups in their portfolios, were each paid at a rate of $5,600 extra for their duties. But by autumn, buffeted by ministers who wanted more help and by backbench Tory M.P.s who wanted the extra experience, prestige, and money, the rookie P.M. had capitulated. The new government would have parliamentary secretaries. (By then the P.M. was even travelling by government JetStar. In September, he returned by JetStar to High River, Alberta, to officially open a new, one-storey building to house the newspaper founded by his grandfather.)

But the anxiety to avoid any image of profligacy endured; once the House sat, the PMO staff was warning cabinet ministers not to leave Ottawa without Joe Clark's personal permission. The ostensible reason was anxiety over non-confidence votes in Parliament; the real reason, said some PMO staff, was concern that the cabinet not seen to be abusing their right to fly about at government expense.

The changeover in offices during that last week before Joe Clark became Prime Minister went smoothly. Clark decided to keep his existing fourth-floor parliamentary office in the Centre Block (it had been Mackenzie King's, and still contained the secret cupboard where King had hidden from unwelcome visitors when he was P.M.). Pierre Trudeau was thus left intact in his third-floor office; only the brass plaques on their doors had to be changed. At the Langevin Block, where the PMO has its command post, arrangements were more complicated. For days the building was filled with boxes being packed and unpacked. For a time, Clark retreated to the Presidential Suite of the Four Seasons Hotel, two blocks away, to conduct his cabinet conversations. He even adopted his own table, number four, in the Four Seasons dining room.

There was the usual jockeying over space. (The clear victor, Jim Gillies, was given the aide's office connecting directly with Clark's.) Security staff at the Wellington Street entrance of the building, facing the Parliament Buildings across the way, finally resorted to taping a set of newspaper photos of the cabinet by their desk, so they could recognize the new boys and stop challenging their right to enter.

The transfer of power was agreed by all to be both amiable and deliberate. (With the possible exception, in respect of amiability, of the Trudeau staffer who left a cardboard sign in a window of the Langevin Building before leaving: "We'll be back," it read. An arriving Clark minion added the words: "That's what the Shah said!") Even the switch of residences was reasonably amiable, although Pierre Trudeau was less than enamoured of the chocolate brown decor Maureen McTeer and her decorator (of whom more in a moment) had inflicted on Stornoway, the official residence of the leader of the opposition. Moreover, the twenty-room mansion had aging plumbing, a population of silverfish, and a platoon of visiting skunks attendant on most garden parties. When the Department of Public Works moved in to renovate, Joe Clark let Pierre Trudeau use the Prime Minister's summer home at Harrington Lake for three weeks during the work period.

Ms. McTeer was equally unimpressed with the brilliant oranges and reds added to the 24 Sussex Drive decor by Margaret Trudeau. She called on her old friend, architect Cecilia Humphreys (wife of Clark's biographer) to help with an austerity redecoration. The reds and oranges were banished from the dining room of the Prime Minister's official residence; but the new P.M. and his wife continued to sleep in a bedroom lined by Maggie Trudeau with canary yellow silk wall covering.

Ms. Trudeau, meanwhile, found time between engagements on movie sets, in magazine editorial offices, and at New York discos to whip into 24 Sussex one sunny day and emerge with the linens she'd ordered specially from Public Works before she became the "estranged" wife of the former P.M. Maggie appropriated the Madeira linen sheets, "with handstitched blue, pink and yellow birds, from London" and the "soft, luxurious towels" the press had just reported Maureen would be inheriting.

When the lint had settled, Maggie had bought a home of her own, just three blocks from Stornoway, complete with, evidently, the Madeira sheets and luxurious towels; the silverfish had been eliminated and the plumbing renovated at Stornoway; and Joe's two-and-a-half-year-old daughter, Catherine, was resuming her swimming lessons in the $200,000 pool built for Pierre Trudeau at 24 Sussex by a group of wealthy Liberal supporters. Later, when questioned in the House of Commons, Clark, unlike his predecessor, provided figures on the public funds spent on such activity:

—The new Prime Minister had spent $30,669.67 fixing up 24 Sussex Drive, (Cecilia Humphreys had told reporters the budget was $15,000.) At his "old" office on Parliament Hill, the P.M. had spent another $19,125, including a "standard, M.P. issue carpet."

—Pierre Trudeau's refurbishing of Stornoway had run to $70,000, including the silverfish; other costs included replacing leaky plumbing, plastering cracked walls and ceilings, and covering that chocolate brown paint Ms. Humphreys and Ms. McTeer had used in the dining room. As for Trudeau's office, renovations and furnishings there had run up a total tab of $86,703.68, but that had all happened back between 1971 and 1974, over a period of three years. The $84,000 limousine was, at least for the moment, in storage.

Harrington Lake was to have a succession of guests over the summer; first Pierre Trudeau was there, perhaps reliving the less troubled days of the late sixties; then, a dashing, bachelor P.M., he'd used Harrington Lake as a private sanctuary for weekend tête-à-têtes with his current lady companion. Then, after his return from Tokyo in June, Joe Clark took Maureen and Catherine to the peaceful Gatineau home.

Later still in the summer, the white, clapboard building housed Lowell Murray, teased out of his Maritime retirement by the offer of a seat in Canada's Senate. Murray stayed at Harrington Lake until his new home, an Ottawa condominium apartment, was ready.

The new members of Parliament were getting house-broken, too. Of the 282 M.P.s elected May 22, 107 were on their first official pilgrimage to the Hill. The House of Commons staff arranged briefings. The freshman members were told about the parliamentary barber shop, the post office, the subsidized cafeteria and dining room ("We encourage you to tip very little. Twenty-five cents has become almost traditional"). There were also the personal parking privileges, the library and research help, and the liquor store handily located in the West Block, a place where M.P.s could actually get their booze via messenger service.

Getting-used-to-things promised to be a major preoccupation. When the Clark cabinet was revealed, only two of its members (not including the Prime Minister) had ever held even a provincial cabinet portfolio. Sixteen years out of office had left the federal Tories thin on experience of government. John Crosbie had served in Newfoundland cabinets, and Solicitor General Allan Lawrence had been Attorney General in Ontario for Bill Davis. James McGrath, named to the Fisheries and Oceans portfolio, had been a parliamentary secretary during John Diefenbaker's term as Prime Minister.

There was a trifle more federal cabinet experience in the Senate, where Joe Clark dipped his line to harvest the Quebec representation he's failed to win in the election. Having first told newsmen he would appoint no more than two senators to his cabinet, Joe Clark found three, including Bob de Cotret. The other two, Martial Asselin (another Minister of State) and Jacques Flynn (Minister of Justice), had both served briefly in Diefenbaker cabinets, Flynn as Minister of Mines and Asselin as Minister of Forestry.

Even more alarming, during the early days, only five members of the first Joe Clark cabinet were given the same portfolios they'd specialized in examining while in opposition. Some of the former opposition critics were simply not named to the cabinet; others were reprogrammed for other niches.

Until the inner cabinet went to Jasper on its spiritual retreat in late August, many of the cabinet were left to function largely on their own. At one of their first meetings, Clark told his ministers to prepare a "work program" giving him the priorities they saw as most urgent in their departments, and deadlines by which they wanted implementation. As a contrast, Margaret Thatcher, elected Conservative Prime Minister of England not long before, had named her cabinet in forty-eight hours, met with its members seventy-two hours after that, and introduced her first budget into the mother of Parliaments within a month. Joe Clark, maybe still bemused by his victory, needed two weeks to identify his cabinet; he waited four and a half months to meet Parliament, and over six months to produce a budget. (As one of their early acts, Parliament and the Senate had to approve special government estimates so federal civil servants could be paid on time; the Parliament of Canada had never been in recess so long in this century.)

Confusion endured for several weeks after the Cabinet was announced. RCMP personnel posted on Parliament Hill shouted at more than one new minister, "You can't park there! That's for the minister!" A parliamentary official assigned to helping new members learn the ropes remarked that "we are not going to hand out beanies, but we thought about it." M.P.s had about as much trouble as reporters finding one another as offices were shuttled, sometimes with bitter feelings when Liberal M.P.s resisted being assigned to some of the Hill's less desirable (tiny) accommodation.

A good deal of the coming and going was observed on T.V. monitors by about the only occupants of the Langevin

Building unaffected by the changes around them. The security squad Mounties assigned to a twenty-four-hour watch on the T.V. screens fed by nine video cameras on the roofs of the Langevin Building and the Parliament Buildings maintained their silent vigil. (One camera, on the Langevin Building, had a 600 mm zoom lens and was, and is, capable of shooting close-up portraits of people standing under the Peace Tower, a quarter-mile away. When there were demonstrations or concerns about "incidents," the cameras would be fed into a bank of video-tape machines, and the pictures preserved for later study.)

Initially, there was fear of a wholesale purge of the senior civil service. If few of the new M.P.s fitted the "slack-jawed, mouth-breather" description once applied to western Tory members by their then colleague, Peter Reilly (who was also one of Canada's finest political journalists), many were, at least, "a bit simplistic," in the description of yet another re-elected Tory M.P. Many of the new backbenchers had been moulded by the hard knocks collected by self-made men and were impatient with "those Liberal mandarins" running the country; they wanted more action, less philosophy, more emphasis on fiscal restraint and less attention to culture, foreign aid, and social programs.

The nervousness in the civil service finally reached such a peak that Joe Clark felt obliged to call forty of the senior bureaucrats to a luncheon at which he spent forty minutes asking for their help and promising them his support. Most left reassured. In the event, the blood bath never occurred. The new P.M. moved softly in the early months. He was aware his new boys would need a lot of expert help.

There was, too, the matter of a very thin mandate. The Liberals after all, had actually gotten more votes than the Tories; the difference had been in huge Liberal majorities (wasted votes, in effect) in Quebec as compared with very thin Tory victory margins in many Ontario seats. A good many people, some of Clark's advisors among them, thought Canadians had not intended to elect a Tory government at all. What the voters had done, they said, was to *defeat* a Liberal government. As if to underline the paucity of Joe Clark's grip on the public will, a Gallup Poll, conducted the very week he was being sworn in as Prime Minister, revealed that only 7 per cent of Canadian voters thought Clark the most effective leader in the country. Sober reading, even at Harrington Lake.

The week after that humiliating poll was taken, but before it was published, Clark told reporter Richard Gwyn that his life had

> been based on a fairly realistic understanding of proba-
> bilities. Now I know about myself that the danger of my
> style of leadership is that it can settle into just keeping
> the ship floating while the problem is to give the ship
> and the crew direction. . . . I've always been realistic
> about this, that there would be no Kennedy or Trudeau
> aura about my early months in office, and that's too bad,
> that the country won't share our enthusiasm.

There was doubt about the leader's "realistic under-standing of probabilities" after the little bluff that failed in December; but Clark's less-than-compelling public presence was an acknowledged fact.

Maybe as a result of his modest self-appraisal as a crowd-mover, the P.M. quickly developed a reputation, among both his colleagues and the Ottawa press corps, of preferring small groups, ideally one-on-one meetings. Reporters noticed that after cabinet meetings ministers descended the elevator in the Langevin lobby, while Clark often used a side elevator taking him to the less-used Confederation Square entrance to the building, thus by-passing the post-cabinet scrum. If Clark came down with the others he usually walked straight across the foyer and on to the corridor leading to the side entrance, ignoring the horde of press and cabinet ministers; if relatively few people were jammed into the lobby and up the staircase he was more likely to pause and answer questions.

With the cabinet, too, he liked face-to-face chats, preferring them to larger gatherings. The smaller, inner cabinet was apparently a more comfortable format, even, than the full cabinet.

In the beginning there was a good deal of time wasted, and communication at all levels was subject to breakdown. One minister complained that early cabinet meetings ran as long as six and seven hours while the Prime Minister patiently allowed members to make, and often repeat, their arguments. He was the "good chairman" everybody had expected of the man who once said, "I've spent the last fifteen years of my life in meetings." But he gave no evidence in June and July of being sure where he wanted to steer the government, and the country.

He was capable of being tough. He'd noted in an interview that toughness, along with innovative skill, came high on his list of preferred qualities in cabinet ministers. "You need some tough-minded people." Providing the example himself, he told one minister: "You're going to have to take the heat for me. You are the one who is expendable. I'm not."

Many of Clark's attempts to make government seem more open and his ministers more approachable foundered or were frustrated. The P.M. told his cabinet to always inform their provincial counterparts of any government decisions or policies affecting the provinces, whether they'd been asked or not. If, once Parliament met, they were asked questions they couldn't answer, they were to say frankly that they didn't know. "And then, find out," added Clark.

But finding things out has always presented some problems in Ottawa. P.C. Party brass were soon echoing the complaints voiced by journalists that reaching cabinet ministers was not an easy task. The ministers' executive assistants

— the folk who generally screen calls and mail to the minister
— were having *their* calls screened by secretaries. And a good
many ministerial secretaries quickly caught onto the notion
that the most prestigious and unanswerable reply when their
minister was unavailable to come to the telephone was to say,
"I'm sorry; the minister is in a cabinet meeting." Unhappily
other Tory M.P.s, even other ministers, generally were aware
the cabinet, however burdened, did not meet *every* day.

Even within the PMO all was not always clear. The Prime
Minister, for instance, had sent the Order-in-Council naming
Robert de Cotret to the Senate to Governor General Edward
Schreyer on June 5, the day after the cabinet was sworn-in.
But a week later reporters calling the PMO for information
were told that "No, Mr. de Cotret hasn't been appointed to
the Senate." The P.R. release hadn't caught up to the event.
On another occasion a reporter called the PMO at about 12:45
P.M. to ask when the weekly cabinet meeting was likely to
finish. "About two o'clock," came the answer. The reporter
turned up at two and discovered the meeting had finished at
12:30 — before the original call.

The P.M. was especially concerned to overcome his
image as a leader chosen only by English Canada. Clark
instructed all those members of his cabinet able to get by in
French — only Flora MacDonald, William Jarvis, and John
Fraser, aside from the Quebec members, Roch LaSalle and
Heward Grafftey — to use the language whenever possible in
public. Even unilingual ministers were told when Parliament
assembled to drop a few French phrases into their speeches;
that way the Tories could ensure a bit more T.V. coverage in
Quebec, something the Liberals were anxious to deny them.
In addition, Clark established simultaneous translation facilities for meetings of both the cabinet and the Treasury Board.
Only Roch LaSalle, of all those present at either, had French
as a first language, but the P.M. wanted the principle under-
lined by example, and often made some of his remarks in

cabinet in French, forcing most of his colleagues to listen to him on English translation earphones. The PMO sent out the word, quietly, that *every* government department was to hire at least one senior, francophone executive.

Nor were ordinary Tory M.P.s exempt from the PMO concern to exhibit well in Quebec. While no press gangs were actually seen in action on Parliament Hill, it was a matter of some surprise that when the House met in the fall one hundred M.P.s, mostly Tories, were in attendance at the French-language lessons made available, free, to members; moreover, about thirty wives of the new Conservative members were along for their lessons, too. (Even senior aide Bill Neville began taking French lessons, two mornings a week, over breakfast in the Chateau Laurier Hotel; and Ron Atkey had francophone staff members put him through French drills by conducting hour-long, mock press conferences in the privacy of his ministerial office suite.)

The Prime Minister kept saying the government was more open, and most people, even most journalists, believed him; the trick, they said, was finding the government. During the first nine weeks of the new order the Prime Minister was out of Ottawa for five weeks. There had been the Tokyo summit for a week in June; on his return there were the two weeks at Harrington Lake, though doubtless surrounded by "those bulging, black briefcases" he'd found awaiting him in the PMO; then, in late July and early August, another two weeks away, touring Africa and attending the Commonwealth conference.

One observer suggested that Clark hadn't yet stopped running for office, hadn't absorbed his victory, didn't feel quite at home unless getting on and off airplanes. Said another, after that poll giving him the confidence, as a leader, of only 7 per cent of Canada's voters: "What easier place to show off your leadership qualities than in some far away country; Japan, say, or Kenya?" There was the notion that, once abroad, a politician can always be presented as a statesman. Still another theory was that Clark, not yet determined on fixed goals, not yet satisfied he had enough data to begin building a budget or legislative program, not yet comfortable with the degree to which his ministers were taking hold, wanted to buy time for all of that to begin to happen. More simply, of course, both the Tokyo and Lusaka conferences were scheduled long before Clark was sworn into office; he just about had to go, though he wasn't obliged to tour other areas in Africa at the cost of an additional week.

It was at about this time that *Globe and Mail* columnist Geoffrey Stevens reported on a man-in-the-street poll he'd conducted in Ottawa. "Nobody really knows what you did at the economic summit in Tokyo," reported Stevens, in an open letter to the P.M. "But most have a vague impression that you performed reasonably well, better than expected." Stevens continued with a sample from his sample: "'I think Clark's doing pretty darned well,' a lady told me the other day. 'You know he's been on holiday for two weeks, don't you?' I said. 'Maybe that's why,' she replied."

The rookie P.M.'s 1979 term of office was never to be entirely free of barbs, jokes, and insults. A few samples:

—In August the Kleinburg, Ontario, Binder Twine Festival (a real event, honestly!) announced a Joe Clark look-alike contest. Newspaper publicity invited photos and entries from anyone who "has an oversized head, large ears and hardly much of a chin."

—That same month a Liberal M.P., formerly in the Trudeau cabinet, said his party would go easy on the new P.M. for awhile. "We don't have to push right now. If we just give Clark enough rope, he'll try to shoot himself."

—A columnist reported that, given new cuff links by Maureen after the election, Clark had gone straight out to have his wrists pierced.

—In Calgary an oilman announced that High River would be unable to celebrate Thanksgiving as "some damn fool sent their turkey to Ottawa."

—And in Ottawa, a member of the PMO staff, taking delivery of a turkey at the Langevin Building, was reported to have told an observer that it was "in case we need spare parts."

The Prime Minister kept his sense of humour, at least in public; the country endured, if with a chuckle; and the *bleuing* of Ottawa continued, though not without a considerable jockeying for the places nearest the salt and a number of deeply bruised egos and ambitions.

For starters, of course, all nineteen cabinet ministers excluded from that inner cabinet felt humiliated. (It was largely to assuage those egos, while pursuing his policy to be more visible in Quebec, that Clark took the entire cabinet to Quebec City for a two-day meeting after returning from the inner cabinet deliberations in Jasper.) There was one step of degradation even below that of belonging to the outer cabinet; that was failure to have been named to any of cabinet's multitudinous committees. Three ministers, Minister of State (for CIDA) Martial Asselin, Minister of State for Social Programs Heward Grafftey, and Minister of State for Fitness and Amateur Sport and Multiculturalism Steve Paproski had achieved that low estate by summer's end, despite the impressive length and tenor of their cabinet titles. Taxed by reporters about having found no home in a single one of the cabinet committees, all three ministers took refuge in the dignity of silence; but each had at least one aide who was permitted to offer the press a comprehensive explanation:

—From the Grafftey office: It was "only partially true" that the minister served on no committees since he had been going along to meetings of the Social and Indian Affairs Committee "on an ad hoc basis."

—From Senator Asselin's office: One of the committees

of which the minister was "not officially a member," that of Foreign Policy and Defence, was one at which "he can be called upon to participate."

—The Hon. Mr. Paproski's staff was more direct and businesslike: A minister would understandably not be on a cabinet committee, they said, "with the heavy workload of his double portfolio."

There were, too, the inevitable bumps between different ministers still unclear, even by autumn, about where one's area stopped and the next began; the inner/outer cabinet system didn't help, nor did some of the arguably make-work appointments, like those of Grafftey and Asselin. They added two Quebec members to the cabinet, and Grafftey, though anglophone, was a veteran of the House, first elected in 1958, and fluently bilingual. But what was a minister in charge of Social Programs to do? Nor was Flora MacDonald likely to make very much room for Asselin, as Minister of State for Canada's International Development Agency — our foreign-aid dispensary — to stretch his political muscles. In fact when major CIDA recommendations went to Treasury Board for approval, they went over the signature and recommendation of Flora MacDonald, not Senator Asselin. (In November, for example, urging an $84-million grant and loan package for a huge irrigation and hydro scheme in Sri Lanka, Flora Mac-Donald appeared personally — and successfully — to secure Treasury Board approval.) Feeling much like the fifth wheels they may well have become, such ministers, hanging tenuously in the thin gravity of the outer ring of satellites spinning around the Prime Minister's office, frequently issued comments and statements which may have been designed as much to remind the P.M. of their presence as to inform or provoke the public.

The boundaries of responsibility weren't any clearer on the economic side of the cabinet. There was no question about who wanted to be the chief spokesman for the govern-

ment on economic matters. His name was John Crosbie/
Sinclair Stevens/Robert de Cotret. But the Finance Minister,
Treasury Board President, and Minister of Economic Devel-
opment and Trade couldn't all do that, or not all at the same
time. But by the time Parliament met it was fair to describe
John Crosbie as the "soldier" of the three. The burly, eloquent
Newfoundlander, who had left his first political boss, Joey
Smallwood, when they differed on policy, chose this time to
stay with the leader of his adopted party. Crosbie shouldered
the party line — and cross — and "took the heat."

Sinclair Stevens carved out his own niche as the cabinet's
chief bureaucrat-basher; and the true Clark acolyte, he
became so fervent in his ardour to break up and sell off
PetroCan and other Crown corporations that he sometimes
seemed more sorcerer's apprentice than good and faithful
servant.

Bob de Cotret courted a low public profile, the antithesis
of both Crosbie and Stevens; he'd had enough heat over his
Senate appointment, just three weeks after his whipping in
the polling booths of Ottawa. But he was the only certifiable
economist among the three; he'd headed the Conference
Board of Canada, a group whose analyses had always pleased
Joe Clark more than those from the rival Economic Council of
Canada. The critical thing, this first year, was to *shape* the
policy; if there was glory in it, Clark would know where it
belonged, and Joe had already demonstrated a sharp memory
and a substantial capacity for gratitude. If there was ignominy,
let Crosbie and Stevens share it.

In August, while the Prime Minister was running out of
ink in Kenya, the chore of bringing order to the conflicting
ambitions, personalities, and spheres of power in the cabinet
was given to Jim Gillies. The economics professor, still on
protracted leave from York University, had a natural kinship
to de Cotret. He also had his own eye on a couple of potential
federal appointments, not least of which was as a successor to

Gerald Bouey, Governor of the Bank of Canada, whose present term in office expired early in 1980. Jim Gillies would go for the solid, Conservative economic approach — the de Cotret hardline. As for making everybody happy while the leader was away, well, it just wasn't a perfect world.

Probably the major paradox underscoring the Tory rule of 1979 was the almost obsessive, Clark-generated drive for consensus in a world where checks, balances, debates and differences of opinion are essential to the machinery. They provide the wheels of government with the traction they need if they are to turn. It's not really grease that makes things go — too much of it only makes them slip and skid. It takes a little sand to stop the wheels spinning — a lesson that the High River Kid should have known from his days of driving Tory candidates through prairie blizzards.

"It used to be that we could go to Ottawa and agree to disagree, and we could do that in a couple of days," said a senior provincial official quoted by columnist Dalton Camp. "But it doesn't work that way now. Even though we disagree on some issue, and will always disagree, we have to keep on meeting; because there's no way those guys in Ottawa are going to admit they disagree with anyone."

The whipsaw between Joe Clark's come-let-us-reason-together approach and the demands of *réal politique* moved back and forth slowly through the summer, but by late autumn that traditional instrument of political torture was moving almost too quickly for the naked (Clark) eye to perceive, its whine apparently beyond the audible cabinet range.

For example, it was abundantly obvious even before the election was called in March 1979, that Ottawa and Alberta were on a collision course on energy policy, particularly on oil prices and the division of the spoils from higher prices. Certainly Alberta Premier Peter Lougheed was in no doubt about that. But Joe Clark, seeking consensus rather than friction offered Lougheed a speedy decision on a new grain terminal wanted at Prince Rupert to move Alberta grain, an earnest of good faith and comradeship.

In a second example, it was clear that there were going to be substantially higher oil prices, and that meant higher inflation; that, in turn, meant hard choices for a government that would feel obliged to restrain labour demands for catch-up wage increases. But Clark scrapped the National Commission on Inflation, a watchdog group set-up by the Liberals and cordially disliked by the Canadian Labour Congress, though it was a thoroughly house-broken, toothless tiger. Now maybe labour would cooperate, too.

Fishing for conciliation seemed to come naturally to Joe Clark much of the time; a sense of timing in respect of when to cut bait seemed foreign to him until, goaded by the record, real and mythical, of flip-flop and weakness, he decided to throw the rod into the lake after the bait, and shoot holes through the bottom of the boat for good measure.

There's a story told about a candidate for county judge in Kentucky. His greatest fear through the campaign was that he'd be forced to take a public position on an issue that had cleanly split his voters: the question of whether the county should pay a bounty on polecats killed by hunters. On the last night of the campaign he was finally confronted with the question at a torch-lit rally.

"Some of my friends, and they are fine people, favour a bounty on pole-cats," said the candidate. "And some of my other friends, and they are fine people, too, and my good friends, oppose the bounty. But unlike my good friend here on the platform with me, and I speak of the yellow-bellied candidate for the opposing party, I am not going to duck this issue, and I'm not going to run from telling you how I feel. There's only one honourable course open in this matter, my good neighbours: I stand, foursquare and forever, with my friends."

The difficulty being that those friends eventually want

to know who *their* friends are. A time would come when consensus wouldn't work and Jim Gillies couldn't help. At that point, a fellow trying to govern by procrastination might end up nursing the polecat himself, with no bounty.

Nor, despite the holiday at Harrington Lake and the time away in Japan and Africa, was there enough time for reflection, for planning. The simple day-to-day exigencies of keeping the country in business were bone-crushing. Clark frequently expressed surprise to reporters that he always found himself taking work home with him at night. Cabinet members told the press of a committee meeting that had run past eleven P.M. and then without completing its agenda.

Even the civil service worried about the work load. Most senior bureaucrats were willing, even eager, to support the aims of the new regime. For openers, the mandarins found Clark and his colleagues far more open to suggestions based on their bureaucratic expertise than the haughty, pressurized group that had turned to Pierre Trudeau for all their intellectual light and warmth. Beyond that, the senior civil service was determined not to be accused again, as they had been during the Diefenbaker years, of deliberately thwarting government policy goals. All of that aside, most key members of Canada's public service have an almost holy dedication to the country and to their work; they want things to go well and they want to be genuinely loyal servants — most of the time. But the cabinet system created at Jasper in June seemed built to punish the most able and energetic ministers — those whose judgement and thoughtful decisions the Prime Minister, the public service, and the country needed most. Saddled in many cases with double portfolios, the ministers in the inner cabinet had, in any event, the most onerous and heavy cabinet tasks already; adding frequent meetings of the inner cabinet to schedules which were mind-bending by themselves could only, and in short order, render the brightest and best impotent and bitter in the face of impossible tasks. Unlike

Trudeau before him, Clark liked to delegate; he saw himself much more as chairman than as operations manager; but his temptation was to delegate too much, to overload strong and willing backs to the breaking point.

By September at least a third of the cabinet were exhibiting the doughy, grey faces of men too long in the pressure cooker without relief. Their speech and mannerisms, even in the casual T.V. scrums after cabinet, were perceptibly less crisp and decisive than a few weeks earlier.

A few took to booze for relief, and a few to irony: Finance Minister John Crosbie, waiting to give reporters a statement in his office after one of 1979's traumatic, Bank of Canada interest-rate hikes, poured himself a glass of scotch and turned to the reporters. He hoisted his glass, said, "Well, here's to the people of Canada. May they survive our first few months in office." He downed the drink, and added, "All right. Where do you want to start?" The tape-recorders had already been started, but the impromptu toast was not broadcast.

A few of the cabinet, most notably Flora MacDonald and Sinclair Stevens, seemed to thrive on the killing pace; they were both where they had always wanted to be, at the centre, wielding power and making decisions; they were having the time of their lives. Even when they were raising hackles, each in his and her own way, they looked comfortable and happy. Joe Clark was blooming, too; he'd been persuaded to drop a habit of jiggling his jowls while orating, had settled into an evidently permanent hair style after three or four changes over the previous year, and found himself occasionally wisecracking with the journalists and T.V. crews who no longer seemed to intimidate him.

Certainly some of the cabinet, and some of the new beneficiaries of Tory largesse, were happy. Roch LaSalle, now master of revels for Quebec patronage plums, seemed more cocky and ebullient than ever. Observers noted that he seemed to have absolute access to the leader anytime he wished it, and that he attended more cabinet meetings, inner and outer, than anyone — although he often spent more time outside the cabinet room (making phone calls, going to the washroom, chatting with reporters, secretaries or anyone else) than any of his colleagues. Ron Atkey was probably surprised and happy, too. Despite his appallingly bad advice to Clark over the Jerusalem embassy move (Atkey was said to have had tears in his eyes, thinking maybe of the next campaign in St. Paul's, when Clark told him of the Stanfield recommendations), he was given a "promotion." Ron Atkey, to the surprise of many Tories, not least Health and Welfare Minister David Crombie, the enormously popular ex-mayor of Toronto, was made "political minister" for Ontario — a kind of anglophone Roch LaSalle. With the federal patronage for Canada's most populous province in his desk, Atkey became one of the most powerful men in Ottawa. He also became, potentially, one who would during the next election, help shape Tory fortunes in Ontario, thereby influencing the fate of the party which desperately needed to hold the gains they'd made in 1979. Without huge inroads into the Liberal power base in Quebec, no Tory government could survive without a majority of Ontario's rich bounty of seats. (There was one plum still to come, on December 31, 1979, when lawyer Atkey was appointed a Queen's Counsel.)

Ottawa civil servants, terrified on May 22 by the prospect of a Tory-run blood bath, could only look back after the fall of the government in December and wonder at the paucity of change. During the spring campaign and before, Joe Clark had said that as Prime Minister he'd demand a *pro forma* resignation from every deputy minister in Ottawa, leaving him free to clear the decks to whatever degree he deemed necessary; Sinclair Stevens, dubbed "Slasher Stevens, the Happy Hacker" by cabinet-wit Crosbie, had left no doubt of the Tory intention to slice 60,000 jobs from the federal civil service.

After the turn-over of office, Stevens added to both the language and the bunker mentality of the civil services with explanations of how he was going "to attrit" the public service. (Had Sinc Stevens fallen into a black hole by September 1979, he would still have earned an eternal place in the history of Canadian literature as the homegrown Sam Goldwyn who had added the precious verbs "privatize" and "attrit" to the lexicon.)

In actuality the cuts were few, and the status was surprisingly quo seven months later. The Liberals had actually reduced the civil service during their last year in office by 3,581. The drop represented only 1.3 per cent of the total federal payroll, but it came close to the jobs eliminated by the fire-breathing new government during its 1979 term of office.

There was to be an additional unemployed "stuffed shirt" of the political persuasion, right after May 22. Madame Tussaud's in London took Pierre Trudeau's effigy back to the storeroom. This was a fair case of Sinc Stevens' attrition, as the Trudeau effigy was not replaced by one of Joe Clark. A spokesman for the world-famed wax museum said it was a small *c* conservative firm, and generally waited until people had built a world reputation before including them in the galleries. No decision on Joe Clark would be made until early 1980, he said — just about as Canadian voters would be recording *their* decision.

The first two victims of Sinclair Stevens "attrit" policy lost their jobs on May 22. That's when two of the Tory's brightest stars, Jean Pigott and Robert De Cotret, were defeated by the Ottawa civil service voters worried about the Sinclair threats to their security. But by early June Ms. Pigott was able to move her collection of fifty porcelain pigs, and her habit of supplying reporters and colleagues with fresh-baked chocolate chip cookies from her family's bakery, to the Prime Minister's office, where she became the PMO's chief advisor on government appointments (read "patronage"). M. de

Cotret, although an Ontario resident, was a francophone and had his cabinet post, via a Senate appointment, before Jean Pigott's porcelain collection had been unpacked. He was to be "our calling card in Montreal and Quebec City," said a flip PMO aide.

The fact that the lady M.P. turned away by Ottawa bureaucrats was now to handle major patronage appointments, or at least recommendations, was only just. There is an intimate of usually invisible relationship between the public service and the partisan goodies doled out by Canadian governments. Many senior government posts are regarded as political spoils, and the lives and careers of civil servants working under those positions are made hard or easy according to the appointments. So the Clark approaches to changes both in the civil service and to patronage appointments were a crucial factor in assessing his skill, even his survival quotient while negotiating the minefields strewn around Ottawa's power bunkers.

So, what about patronage? More or less what one might expect, was the verdict of old Ottawa hands after the seven months of Tory rule; some of it respectable, some of it inevitable, a bit of it rather more greedy and gauche than one might have hoped. But, in the words of a *Toronto Star* editorial, it was mostly just a case of "new hands at the public udder."

Political charity, like most, begins at home. So it began with Jean Pigott, Jim Gillies, Robert de Cotret, and the rest. John Crosbie, who had asked two veteran Ottawa journalists to consider being his press secretary was approached quietly but firmly by the PMO; he hired defeated Eglinton M.P. Rob Parker, instead. Clark himself added two failed Tory candidates from Quebec, Andre Payette and Pierrette Lucas, to his own press entourage. By early autumn he would also rescind his earlier ban on parliamentary secretaries, adding twenty-two P.C. backbenchers to the "bonus" payroll list.

Another defeated Tory M.P. Yuri Shymko, from Toronto's

Parkdale riding, found safe haven as an assistant to Steve Paproski. Even a former Liberal M.P., Ralph Stewart, who had crossed the floor to join the Conservatives just three weeks before the spring election was "remembered." Stewart, who had been kept employed as a special advisor to Joe Clark between the dissolution of the House in March and the candy parade in September, was hired on September 25 as Canada's new consul-general to Atlanta, Georgia.

Nobody expressed great surprise at the appointments; they were, however cynical, a part of the Canadian political tradition of payment for services rendered. When Lowell Murray was appointed to the Senate in October, he under-lined the sanctity of the hard-played partisan game in his maiden speech: "Political partisanship is the foundation not just of our electoral system but of our parliamentary process and of our democratic system," said the youthful Senator.

One of his rapt listeners was Senator Keith Davies, the former Liberal campaign chairman who, like Murray, had been put on hold in the Senate by a grateful (and victorious) Prime Minister. Murray made no mention of the personal hardships sometimes accompanying the reception of party largess. In his own case the sacrifice had involved a move to Ottawa; this because the Prime Minister had appointed Murray as a representative from Ontario, although Murray was a Maritimer and harboured a cordial dislike for most of Ontario and, as the proper habitat of a civilized person, Ottawa in particular. But Joe Clark needed the Maritime Senate vacancies to bestow on other folk; and besides there were some old-line Tories in New Brunswick and Nova Scotia who weren't all that fond of young Lowell and would have taken his appointment from their area to be an unkind gesture.

The High River hustler saw himself, above all, as a poli-tical creature. He'd never disavowed the practice or principle of patronage during his fifteen-plus years of party work. Indeed, just as Lowell Murray had called with suggestions for

cabinet and other appointments from pay stations while fishing in New Brunswick in June, Joe Clark had often bombarded
the P.C. party brass, in his youth, with similar suggestions
about people "deserving" jobs. Roch LaSalle had set the tone,
soon after his own appointment: "I don't intend to pass up our
opportunity," he said. LaSalle added that there was no question of his plans to award government contracts to party
supporters in his home province in hopes of enhancing future
Tory prospects in Quebec.

Questioned about the LaSalle comments at the Jasper
meeting of the inner cabinet, Clark told reporters the M.P.'s
statements were "an astute observation of the political history
of Quebec." Presenting the half-smile that usually lit up one
side of his face when he felt he'd worked out just the right
reply, he added: "Certainly we are going to ensure in a
reasonable way, a way that maintains propriety, that activities
undertaken by the Conservative government do not benefit
the Liberal Party. . . . The problem in the past has been that in
certain cases it has not been enough for a Conservative to be
competent. It has been necessary for him to be a Liberal. I
naturally am not going to exclude from consideration Canadians who happen to share [both] competence and my political
affiliation." Circumlocutionary perhaps, but clear.

Jean Pigott was more direct: "What's wrong with patronage?" she asked.

Roch LaSalle had a further sally. Prominent Liberals
previously appointed to major posts should resign, he said.
"Their honesty should compel them to resign." They could
then be replaced by Tories, "and *they* would know how to give
the most loyalty to the government."

Environment Minister John Fraser was equally candid.
He was going to draw up a list of lawyers suitable to do
government work, he announced, "and suitable means Conservative."

Jean Pigott, meantime, was trying to collect a list of the

public service sanctuaries within the grasp of the PMO. It took awhile. Early requests to Crown corporations and government boards to find out exactly which positions were vacant, or would be, went unanswered in many cases. But Joe Clark's "human resources director" owned the muscle; she had a sharp note from the Prime Minister sent to the foot-draggers. Soon she'd assembled four yellow loose-leaf binders listing the hundreds of government appointments controlled through the P.M.'s office. Many existing appointments still had months, even years, to run; but lots of prizes were there for the taking right now, and there would be more, every week.

There were a lot of executive assistants and aides still to be appointed, too. Including Mark Lyons, a cousin to Clark's friend (and Metro Toronto fund-raiser) Jeff Lyons; and there was the son of Defence Minister Allan McKinnon, one of the first men to approach Joe Clark urging that he contest the leadership, and the only member of the Ottawa Tory caucus who'd fought by Clark's side throughout that campaign. (One T.V. journalist said of McKinnon: "He's the sort of cabinet minister who, when you see him coming down the corridor, you turn off the camera lights and send the film crew on a coffee break.") But McKinnon was Clark's unabashed and uncritical fan; and Joe gave loyalty where he found it: reciprocity was what mattered.

Other debts were paid: Richard Janelle, the Socred M.P. who deserted his rump party to beef up Tory ranks and votes in the House was made parliamentary secretary to Elmer Mackay, the Minister of Regional Economic Development; the appointment brought more than an extra $5,600 per year in the pay envelope: the Mackay portfolio was itself a prime conduit for dispensing patronage plums in Quebec, and as parliamentary secretary, Janelle could help place the goodies where they would best be calculated to turn the Social Credit seats of 1979 into Tory ridings in the next election.

In Ontario two of the first four judges appointed in September to Canada's non-political bench had been in May campaign managers for successful Tory candidates.

In October Jean Casselman Wadds, a Conservative M.P. between 1958 and 1968, was appointed High Commissioner to London, replacing the retiring Liberal doyen Paul Martin, who had been no slouch himself in succeeding Liberal cabinets at engineering friendly employment services. Mrs. Wadds and Joe Clark had worked on Conservative campaigns together as far back as the fifties.

The appointments didn't end with the life of Parliament in December. The day after Boxing Day, 1979, Don Hamilton, the May campaign manager in British Columbia for the Conservatives, was named to head Loto Canada and oversee distribution of the $24 million it would get annually from Canada's provinces.

While he was appointing parliamentary secretaries in October, Clark had also taken the opportunity to make good on a campaign promise and to correct a blunder. Energy Minister Ray Hnatyshyn, who had been agonizing under the twin portfolios of Energy, and Science and Technology — a Liberal heritage that the Prime Minister had promised in the campaign to divide into two full departments — was relieved of his Science portfolio. It was given to Heward Grafftey, and Grafftey's first job, that of administering the phantom department of Social Programs, was abolished. No one missed it. (Later, PetroCan was also subtracted from Hnatyshyn's faltering grasp, and given to Michael Wilson.)

Taken overall, Jean Pigott had come a long way from handing out chocolate chip cookies.

There were government contracts, too: Allan Gregg had been responsible during the 1979 election campaign for conducting private polls for the Conservatives. At the end of May, immediately after the returns, the twenty-seven-year-old Gregg set up a new company, Decima Research Limited, in Toronto. Before the year's end, Gregg's new firm had landed two government contracts totalling $151,000, the largest, for $101,000, having been awarded without benefit of a tender. When Liberal M.P. Robert Kaplan described the deals as a case of "straight patronage," Gregg responded by describing Kaplan as "a silly dink." The contracts stood.

John Crosbie, who'd also been a Finance Minister in Newfoundland, and had been given post-graduate exposure to patronage under Premier Joey Smallwood, put his money where his votes were. Just a week after being sworn to office on June 4, Crosbie announced a grab-bag of Newfoundland projects with a total price tag of $57 million. The goodies covered construction of a drydock, expansion of a liner board mill, development of an industrial park, and extension of the highway system.

Probably the silliest (and most expensive) pay-off involved a campaign promise nobody particularly wanted to keep. The Liberal government's avowed intention to decentralize Ottawa's bureaucracy had, for several years, included plans to move the headquarters of the Department of Veteran's Affairs to Prince Edward Island. Most veterans didn't like the idea; neither did the Canadian Legion, nor, most of all, the Ottawa employees of the department. The P.E.I. location had been selected when a Liberal Minister of Veterans' Affairs (then a member for P.E.I.) approved the move in 1976. But nothing much had been done. David MacDonald, soon to be State Secretary and Communications Minister in the Clark government, was not enthusiastic about the move. Because Canada's population of war veterans was aging rapidly, there'd probably be no reason to have a department for them at all by 1990 or shortly after; and the move would be expensive, costing anywhere from $40 million to $80 million. But the Tories wanted (and won) those four Prince Edward Island seats in May. Joe Clark, who firmly backed the move during the campaign, ordered it implemented after the election. His good friend, Defence (and Veterans' Affairs) Minister Allan

McKinnon, like John Crosbie, was a good soldier in the Clark legions. It would be done, and damn the newspaper ink, rebellious Ottawa staff, and sundry political grapeshot. "If you are sitting back and thinking rationally why this is happening, it's pretty hard to get it to fit a pattern. If you put it into the politics of the last three years, you can see why it's happening." (That last from David MacDonald, one of the most universally admired and respected members of the Clark cabinet of 1979.)

At the same time the P.E.I. move was being approved, as one of nine that he said were "too pregnant" to be stopped, Treasury Board President Sinclair Stevens was happily telling Canadians, on July 27, that the government was going to save $200 million by scrapping or delaying nineteen other moves in the former Liberal package for decentralization. In yet another of his contributions to the articulation of political policy, Stevens said the concept of decentralization was "perhaps desirable, but mostly symbolical (sic)."

Meanwhile, the Ottawa civil service was acquiring a collective stiff neck from trying to watch for the descent of the Big Stick while fascinated with the dispensation of all those lovely carrots. There had been stories during the campaign, often from prominent Conservatives, of a civil service hit-list; and there were all those Stevens promises to "cut the fat" and develop "lean government services." The public, after all, loved to bitch about bureaucrats almost as much as about the CBC or the telephone system; and the press always found them a convenient whipping boy. Besides, Sinc Stevens had told the public he could sweat $2 billion from the government payroll by "attriting" 60,000 public servants. This, he said, because every federal employee gone would save taxpayers around $20,000 per year. Mind you, government surveys showed that 80 per cent of civil servants were in low-wage categories, but Sinc was including savings in office space, stationery, phone calls, and typewriter ribbons. Also, if the full savings of $20,000 annually were realized, and if every one of the 60,000 jobs Sinc thought he could drop was actually eliminated, that would only bring about a total cut of $1.2 billion, not the $2 billion he'd pledged. But no one expected Treasury Board Presidents to have to occupy themselves with arithmetic.

Stevens had imposed a two-month freeze on the civil service, from mid-June until August 15; and he pulled a savage end-run in early August: he instructed all deputy ministers, by telex, that they were forbidden to fill any civil service jobs that had been vacant for six months or more. All such jobs, as of August 11, were eliminated, said the telex. Nevermind that many jobs had been left open through the election period (since March) to await the policies of a new government; never mind that some jobs were awaiting specialized people who were temporarily unavailable; kill those positions. A few mandarins reportedly tried end-runs of their own: They pre-dated job offers to a few days before receipt of the telex. Most didn't.

Some people, mostly those on short-term government contracts, did lose their jobs when the summer "freeze" prevented their re-employment at the end of a contract period. A few more lost job opportunities through the six-month-elimination rule. But the early cries of anticipated agony from leaders of the civil service union, the Public Service Alliance of Canada, were muted by autumn; things were going to be all right, after all.

So with the putative blood bath of senior mandarins. It looked more like a shaving scratch when the smoke had cleared. While there likely had never been a real Tory hit list, a couple of major figures were slated to go — and they went. One was Michael Pitfield, who had been too good a friend to Pierre Trudeau; the other, Central Mortgage and Housing chief Bill Terron was just too good a Liberal. There were a few more resignations, and a few more firings:

—Sylvia Ostry, chairman of the Economic Council of Canada, quit to work for the OECD in Brussels. She said the job offer overseas was "coincidental" in its timing; but fortunate. She'd not have worked happily under the gaze of Bob de Cotret.

—T. K. Shoyama left his job as chairman of Atomic Energy of Canada Limited. Shoyama was reportedly upset by the ousting of his good friend (and successor in his former job as deputy minister of Finance). That friend was fired. He was:

—William Hood, regarded as not sufficiently flexible or imaginative to serve John Crosbie. To replace him, Crosbie brought in Grant Reuber, a Conservative advisor during the opposition years.

—Gordon Robertson, secretary to the cabinet for federal-provincial relations, also left quietly. He wrote, accurately, to Joe Clark that his labours for the Trudeau government had, "identified me in a personal way with former policies and former governments to a degree that could embarrass your efforts to establish your own approach."

—And there was Bryce Mackasey, fired from his $90-thousand-a-year job as chairman of Air Canada. The former Trudeau cabinet minister and (more recently) failed federal candidate, kept his $38,000 pension, and was given a golden handshake in six figures since the Tories could find no legal way to avoid it. But he was gone, and with him the Conservative rage over one of the most blatant examples of a Liberal patronage appointment.

Remarkably, one man most expected to be fired was kept on. Deputy Energy Minister Ian Stewart had been assumed to be due for the high jump, given Tory dedication to developing their own energy policy. But Stewart had been the man who briefed Joe Clark for his Tokyo summit talks on energy; Clark had credited his decent showing in Japan in part to Stewart; and Stewart was to stay.

Similarly with Bernard Ostry, Sylvia's husband and a long-term Liberal appointee. Previously a CBC officer, Bernie Ostry had been Undersecretary of State and then had headed Canada's Museums Board before becoming Deputy Minister of Communications. Regarded as a loyal Liberal servant, Ostry nonetheless proved himself almost instantly irreplaceable to David MacDonald. The two had been friends before the Tory victory, and MacDonald had no intention of losing one of the most creative mandarins in the Ottawa service.

So by the year's end, the predictions had been denied, and the expectations turned inside out. It was not the bureaucracy that had been pared, nor the mandarins who had been purged. Rather it was the government itself that had been destroyed and scattered across the land, seeking re-employment. The Clark government had not failed ostentatiously in its Ottawa constituency, as it was to do in Parliament, but it had failed to leave more than a few scuffs and scratches on the smooth veneer of the capital city. Its passage had been swift, its life short, and its impact slight.

As we shall see now, much the same might be said of the government stage farthest from Camelot-on-the-Rideau — in the global theatre.

~ 6 ~

Foreign Affairs:
Playing in the Major Leagues

At its pragmatic best, the practice of foreign policy by any state requires a mix of high principle and low cunning. Foreign ministers, like the Roman god Janus, guardian of heaven, should have two faces: one, a Pollyanna countenance radiant with good thoughts and expectations, for domestic relations; and another, expressing an auctioneer's shrewdness and a whore's calculation, for those met around international bargaining tables. Joe Clark's 1979 government did little to build Canada's slim global repute either as hooker or horse-trader.

There had been easier times: 105 years earlier Toronto's *Globe* newspaper had editorially celebrated the fact that "We could not be freer than we are now, for we have no foreign policy to complicate things."

By 1979, history buffs, looking to Canada's failed nuclear reactor sales in Latin America and Asia, might have thought Sir Clifford Sifton was closer to the mark when he wrote in the *Canadian Historical Review* in 1922 that "Our external relations are wrapped in what might be called a highly luminous but cloudy halo."

The halo had slipped a few times since 1922 and its luminosity had taken on new meaning when, on May 18, 1974, Indira Gandhi's scientists exploded a test atom bomb built from plutonium produced in a Canadian nuclear reactor. Mrs. Gandhi, herself still in political purdah in the spring of 1979, was nonetheless continuing to influence Canadian policy abroad. The telegram sent to the Indian Prime Minister in 1974 signalling successful firing of the subcontinent's first "peaceful nuclear device" (a description about as valid as that of a "philanthropic loan shark" or a "sterile conception") said: "The Buddha is smiling." The obscene irony implicit in using the name of the prophet of peace to describe completion of the most hideous engine of war yet conceived was not much greater than that surrounding Canada's nuclear policy in the thirty years plus prior to 1974. Canada had been an intimate participant in Hiroshima, by way both of research and raw (uranium) material. Later, in Lester Pearson's pious pilgrimages to Washington, the P.M. would claim Canadian uranium sold to the U.S. was for peaceful purposes only. The Americans didn't much care; it all went into the same inventory — some for bigger and better "nukes," some for cobalt bombs and medical tracers.

When Canada developed the CANDU nuclear reactor generating system in the early sixties, we began trying to export the "safest" and "most peaceful" form of atom energy, unmindful, mostly, that CANDU's by-product, plutonium (one of the most toxic substances ever identified, with a half-life of 35,000 years) was itself the basic building block and fuel for nuclear weapons. It all reminded one of Oscar Levant's remark that he had "known Doris Day before she was a virgin."

Although India had bought its uranium from Britain, and its processing know-how from France, the research reactor that produced the plutonium necessary to build the Indian bomb was a Canadian contribution to the project; and Canada had signed a nuclear non-proliferation treaty way back in 1969, five years before the Gandhian magic mushroom poisoned our international image, and four years before, in 1973, we agreed to sell a CANDU reactor to Argentina, with no control strings whatsoever attached to the deal. Canada's government was hugely embarrassed by the Indian atomic test and resultant world criticism; the then opposition party, the Progressive Conservatives, weren't kind to Mr. Trudeau's regime in discussing the matter in Parliament.

But CANDU, the world's only power-generating reactor that had successfully produced electricity on a commercial scale using natural uranium and heavy water (instead of the less stable and more expensive "enriched" uranium used by other systems) was a major factor in Canada's global trade aspirations. With per-unit costs running upwards of $300 million (for a 600-kW station) and Canada well ahead of competitors in the world market, the CANDU was regarded as a hallmark of Canadian technical sophistication and a saviour of Canadian jobs. So Canada, it was decided in 1974 (one year after signing that contract with Argentina), would impose contractual "safeguards" on future CANDU sales. We'd make sure future buyers didn't follow Gandhi's noisy example.

Those twin anxieties, the desire to make a very large buck without playing nuclear pimp to some potentially unstable nation itching for an atomic orgasm, still bedevilled Canadian foreign policy when Joe Clark took office June 4. But Joe, off to the Tokyo summit after becoming P.M. had the chance to play virtuous salesman. Japan had been "considering" purchase of four CANDU reactors for a considerable time. Japan's Trade Department seemed to want to make the billion-dollar-plus purchase, but that nation's Atomic Energy Commission was less zealous; sure, Japan imported 99 per cent of all its petroleum and was already the world's second-largest user of nuclear energy, producing 10 per cent of all its vast, industrial power requirement from its nineteen reactors; but continuing to buy off-the-shelf technology could only delay Japan's necessary development of its own technology, argued the atom chiefs. (In fact the Japanese Atomic Commission chairman, Iwazo Kaneko, had told his Trade Department in April that the CANDU buys were a bad idea. Instead of adding CANDU to its chain of U.S.-designed, light-water reactors, Japan should accelerate its own heavy-water/natural-uranium research, he said.) Canadians probably knew, by June, that the Trade officials in Japan were at best barely staving off demands that the negotiations be cancelled. Atomic Energy of Canada Limited's international president, Ross Campbell, was a former Canadian ambassador in Tokyo and undoubtedly had good contacts in the Japanese capital. But Joe Clark was encouraged, as part of his Japanese initiation to the mechanics of summitry, to speak for what was already a dying cause. The kid from High River could be skewered by ex-diplomats as well as his own staff and cabinet colleagues, it developed.

Joe went off, all obliging smiles and high hopes. Before a forty-five-minute meeting with Prime Minister Masayoshi Ohira, Clark told Canadian reporters, "I plan to indicate personally to the Prime Minister of Japan the very real importance to Canada of the CANDU sale." The current Canadian ambassador in Tokyo, Bruce Rankin, said he hoped the Clark/Ohira chat would give "added impetus" to flagging Japanese interest in CANDU. Three days later, on June 30, Joe Clark was beaming after a second CANDU sales pitch, this one to Trade Minister Masumi Esaki. It was like preaching to the converted at Easter service; Esaki wanted the CANDUs, but, as Ross Campbell must have known, it was atom boss Kaneko who would make the final judgement, and Kaneko was the one player of the three key Japanese whom Clark did not see. Never mind.

"We're back in the ball game," beamed Clark, after his

meeting with Esaki. The fellow who'd been described as a youth with his head full of baseball statistics, and who loved to study sports, but not to participate, stayed with the metaphor: "We just don't know what inning we're in," he said, and added, "There is no doubt this deal could open the door to Pacific trading countries in the area of high technology." Ambassador Rankin, backed into a corner by the press, agreed that the meeting "improved our chances."

In fact, Canada had a couple of aces to play in the table stakes game: Japan would need a hell of a lot of uranium in coming years, and we had it — to sell or withhold. Japan was also bleeding for oil, but had capital to burn; and Canada was anxious for capital to develop the Alberta tar sands, which had oil potential enough for both our nations. But nobody had urged the Prime Minister to raise or call; poker wasn't his game, and these were "friendly" talks.

The result was predictable. Six weeks later, to revert to Joe Clark's metaphor, the game was over. Atom Commission chief Kaneko announced on August 10 that Japan was not going to proceed with any plans to buy CANDU. Hardball evidently wasn't our game. But, by persuading the P.M. to pinch hit, Canada's AECL boss-salesman, Campbell, had avoided having to strike out himself in a game played under the lights. Clark would have to share blame for the shut-out. (Campbell was actually in Tokyo, the day of the Kaneko announcement. He had no comment.)

More was to come: Canada had a contract with Argentina made in 1973, you'll recall, to sell that nation a CANDU reactor. The price tag, in 1973, had been $320 million; the target date for completion of the generating plant had been 1980; the safeguards imposed by Canada on the Argentinians had been nil. In 1974 Canada asked for some guarantees from Argentina, which was one of six nations in the world believed capable of developing atomic weapons but which had refused to sign the non-proliferation treaty. Argentina agreed to the guarantees.

In 1976 the Trudeau government juggled the safeguard deal some more and the Argentinian government went along. By now the Latin Americans were talking about at least four reactors, and were negotiating with Canada for their second plant, with more out there in the future.

There were some hitches, and some questions. The questions:

—Why did Argentina, with more than 90-per-cent oil self-sufficiency and huge hydro resources lying undeveloped, have such a hankering for massive nuclear power development?

—How stable were relations between the military regime in Argentina and that in her rival for primacy in South America, Brazil?

—Why hadn't Argentina (or Brazil) signed the nonproliferation treaty, promising not to build atom bombs?

—Was Argentina's often repressive and occasionally belligerent junta the sort of government we wanted to help produce pure plutonium?

The problems:

—The original CANDU contract had been, after a few renegotiations, swollen beyond recognition. It was now going to cost the Argentinians somewhere between $1.1 billion dollars and $1.3 billion (instead of $320 million) and the plant wouldn't be feeding power into that country's grid before March 1982 at the earliest (instead of 1980 at the latest).

—There had been a very messy scandal associated with the first CANDU contract in which it developed that AECL had provided money into seven figures (millions) for "expedition" (bribes) to help seal the contract.

—Even with the new price tag of over a billion dollars, the Argentina CANDU sale had turned out to be a loss leader; after all the bills were paid, Canadian taxpayers would be forced to pick up a loss of not less than $130 million on the deal, more than a third of the original asking price.

But we sure wanted that second contract, by golly. There was some opposition in Canada. On July third, just as Joe, Maureen, and Catherine were settling into that well-deserved holiday at Harrington Lake, picketers at Saint John, New Brunswick, temporarily blockaded loading of an Argentina-bound ship carrying heavy water. The protestors said Canada should, first, ask Argentina to free a few thousand imprisoned trade unionists, restore civil rights, and sign the non-proliferation treaty. Next day, a group of clergy and trade union spokesmen met Flora MacDonald in Ottawa, to press the point. Ontario Federation of Labour human rights director Don Lee told reporters Miss MacDonald had said Canada must and would honour its commitment to build the first CANDU in Argentina. He was pessimistic about tougher safeguards on any potential future sales.

Meanwhile, back at the PMO's corral, a summer's contest was shaping up between the "doves" and the "hawks." The hawks, headed by Trade Minister Robert de Cotret and International Trade Minister Michael Wilson, stated a simple case:

—CANDU was Canada's showcase, one shining example of global, technical leadership; it was our paid passage out of the industrial backwoods, our clear opportunity to stop spending all our time hewing wood and drawing water.

—Our international balance of trade was awful. And CANDUs cost one hell of a lot of money. We needed to make a sale. Besides, AECL said Canada had to sell an average of one CANDU annually to keep our nuclear power infrastructure from fading away.

—The CANDU research and development industry meant jobs, about 35,000 of them, according to AECL. What's more, almost 90 per cent of those jobs were in Ontario.

(Don't forget that Bill Davis, struggling with a sluggish industrial economy and a minority Tory government of his own, had been a hell of a lot of help back there in April and May.) Nor do *we* want to see people unemployed and an industry run down our first year in office 'cause we missed the bus.

—If we don't sell Argentina CANDUs, somebody else will sell them nuclear know-how.

Flora MacDonald was leader of the doves; she had support, vocal or inferred, from David MacDonald, David Crombie, and Ron Atkey. Their arguments were clear:

—We don't want another India. No further explanation needed.

—The safeguards need to be reviewed. Argentina should be pressured to sign the treaty. (Environment Minister John Fraser was soon to announce a review for 1980 of all matters relating to nuclear energy, including CANDU sales and safeguards; he didn't expect the icy December douche, either.)

—We want "clean" sales; no more of those bribes.

—Argentina is not a very nice country. Her government's record on civil liberties was widely condemned. It is very easy to obtain long-term accommodation in her jails, without the fuss of habeas corpus or trial. Not so easy to get out, even assuming your friends and relatives know where you are, and can find a lawyer bold enough to espouse your cause.

—Argentina and Brazil are contending for power on that huge continent; probably both think a small nuke would rattle a lot more effectively than any of the sabres they now have in the arms lockers.

It was a chairman's verdict, a compromise of sorts: we would ask for safeguards, even speak out on civil rights; but we would go after that sale!

On September 11 Michael Wilson went after that sale.

After a Calgary Canadian Club luncheon speech, he flew south bearing a letter from Joe Clark to Argentinian President Jorge Videla. Wilson met, too, with the man running the country's nuclear energy project, Rear-Admiral Carlos Castro Madero. Clark's message: there would be "no more surprises" from Canada regarding nuclear safeguards. (We'd go on playing softball, with maybe an occasional overhand pitch.)

Said Wilson, verging on departure (and maybe desperation): "If the contract is not signed now, $1.8-billion worth of business will be lost, and 50,000 to 60,000 Canadians now employed in the nuclear industry rely on that export business." (The total people employed had grown rapidly from AECL's 35,000; but who expects cabinet ministers to check the figures.)

Rear-Admiral Madero was to say, just three weeks later, that he had "appreciated the openness of the dialogue with Mr. Wilson." But Mike Wilson in Buenos Aires, like Joe Clark in Tokyo, was pinch-hitting in a hopeless cause. It was top of the ninth; there were two out; nobody was on base; and Wilson had a broken bat, whatever AECL had told him before his departure about its hickory construction.

Argentina already had one other nuclear reactor, a small, pilot project built by the Germans; it had been finished on time, and at the cost originally contracted for. And in 1976, when the Trudeau government for a time instructed AECL to suspend negotiations for more Argentine sales until that country agreed to broader nuclear safeguards, Argentina hired the German group, for $2 million, on a special project. The Germans were to reassemble the designers who had built the small, heavy-water reactor, and produce designs for a full-scale, 600-megawatt version, like CANDU. There may have been what the football players, at contract time, call "added inducements." Germany, not having been caught greasing palms in the past, might be a more compliant business partner; Germany had been a shade less publicly critical of

Argentina's major growth industry — the prison system; and Germany's requirements on safeguards were less stiff than Canada's.

No professional gambler, assessing those odds, would have bankrolled Mike Wilson's Buenos Aires plane fare. All of the foregoing data was known before the International Trade Minister lifted off from Calgary International Airport. What Wilson didn't know — and his Latin hosts were too polite to spoil his trip by telling him — was that having already negotiated a deal with Germany their government had put the Argentinian memo-writing machine into gear, and it was, even now, producing the paper missile that would shoot down AECL's latest dream castle. But Latin American bureaucratic presses grind no more quickly than those in Ottawa; well before the press release was ready, AECL was to find a *post facto* scapegoat in Manhattan.

First, though, Mike Wilson took time to paint the hard line in bold colours, and send the doves back to their coop. He would not, said Wilson, await establishment of John Fraser's all-party parliamentary committee probe of CANDU sales before signing a new deal with Argentina. (Parliament, it turned out, wouldn't wait, either.) He, Wilson said, would not risk losing the CANDU sale while waiting for a committee; but the government would insist on "nuclear monitoring."

But about the scapegoat: Flora MacDonald, out to polish the world's Biggest Apple, was taking her ease in a New York hotel suite and talking with *Toronto Star* reporter Stephen Handleman on September 24. Mike Wilson was just tapering off his lomotil therapy and getting used to the luxury of drinking tap water without apprehension. Flora was musing, while Handleman took notes, about nuclear proliferation and about human rights. MacDonald was getting her head in gear for her United Nations debut that evening; Handleman was getting a juicy by-line story; Ross Campbell, though he didn't know it yet, was getting his fall person.

"Canada will take a hard line toward the six countries who are believed to have the capacity to develop nuclear weapons but have not signed the nuclear non-proliferation treaty," Handleman reported next day. The six were: "Pakistan, India, Israel, South Africa, Brazil and Argentina." (*That* wasn't the sort of hard line de Cotret and Wilson had in mind, at all.)

The *Star* reporter continued, quoting Canada's Secretary of State for External Affairs directly: "'I see Canada not having any further extension of facilities to them unless they come under that umbrella and agree to full investigation of everything they have.'" Flora MacDonald said, adding, "'that even stricter safeguards are expected [from the Fraser committee] to be recommended in February.'" And there was more, from Miss MacDonald: "'The question of what we do in nuclear technology, where we export it, what conditions we place on it — what is the political stability of that country — and what are the goals of that country should be part and parcel of any condition of export.'" Moreover, said Handleman: "Miss MacDonald said the country will concentrate on areas of the world where it can use its clout, such as Latin America and the Caribbean, and on policy areas where it has special leverage, such as nuclear exports and foreign aid." That was Monday evening.

Tuesday, at the U.N., Flora impressed her new colleagues with a passionate, thirty-five-minute plea for a return to the basic human rights issues which underlay the United Nations' reason for being. Flora told the delegates:

We have lost our grasp of the human needs that the United Nations was established to fill and of the human rights that it was meant to protect. . . . These crimes against humanity are common knowledge. Too often, the political convenience of governments has caused them to remain silent when ordinary people cried out for action.

Miss MacDonald had examples: South Africa, Zimbabwe, Namibia, Cambodia, Laos and Vietnam; Equatorial Guinea, where 50,000 were reported killed by Francisco Marcias Nguema; the Central African Republic, where tyrant Jean-Bédel Bokassa held cannibalistic feasts and murdered 200 school children; Uganda and the blood-drenched Amin regime; *and Argentina, "where 4,000 people have disappeared."*

Flora was widely congratulated at the U.N. In Canada, where the speech had been telecast live, it struck responsive chords from millions of voters and hit one sour note — at AECL headquarters. Six days later, on Monday, October 1, the Argentinians finished their memo and delivered it. It said that Germany, not Canada, was going to build their next reactor. Oblivious to the fact that the German-Argentine pact had obviously been under negotiation for months and settled for weeks, atomic industry spokesmen called Flora's interview and speech the straw that broke the camel's back. The Argentinians had been reassured by the Wilson mission, the spokesmen said; then, in the words of one nuclear industrialist, one without the temerity to let his name be used: "Flora mouths off with her morals and dancing and angels on the head of a pin and all that. What would you do if you were the Argentines?" What indeed? Hire a ghost-writer, maybe.

Ross Campbell of AECL told a reporter on Tuesday, October 2, that "Argentina seemed ready to buy the reactor until Miss MacDonald told a Canadian journalist after her U.N. speech that Argentina is one of a few countries responsible for significant violations of human rights." (His context was as confused as the previous critic's syntax; she'd told the whole world, on television, from the podium of the United Nations General Assembly.) Mr. Campbell also blamed the loss of the CANDU sale on the government's "waffling" over nuclear safeguards, and its failure to assure the Latin Americans the rules "wouldn't be changed again."

Mr. Campbell, said the *Globe and Mail* story, was "visibly

bitter about the Argentine defeat [and] complains that AECL seems incapable of getting 'consistent government support' to market CANDU at home or abroad." (This after two sales pitches by the Prime Minister himself, and that later occasion when the P.M. had Michael Wilson try spitting into the prevailing wind over the pampas.)

Confusion, of course, is contagious. Canadians trying to sort out the issue were never even to know the length of the statement from Argentina. It was either

—"a 26-page document" (*Toronto Star*, October 2);

—"the 29-page statement" (*Globe and Mail*, October 4);

—"Argentina's 18-page statement" (*Toronto Star*, October 4, news page story);

—"the 26-page statement" (*Toronto Star* columnist Richard Gwyn, October 4, on a different page); or

—"an 18-page statement" (*Toronto Star*, October 5).

And the overall Argentine nuclear program was now likely going to total "$10 billion" (Richard Gwyn in the *Star*, October 4) or maybe "$15 billion" (the *Star*, October 5).

But it was clear that the Argentinian statement itself did give valid reasons for turning down the CANDU; they boiled down, in the main, to AECL bungling of schedules and costs. There was also the fact that the German reactor yielded more work in sub-contracts within Argentina than the CANDU, said the document. The more lax German safeguard system got no mention, but there was an elliptical reference in the text of the statement: "One of the considerations . . . was . . . that awarding . . . contracts to the same supplying country might handicap capacity to develop an *independent program less subject to possibilities of external interference*."

When, just twenty-four hours after Parliament met to hear the Throne Speech, an opposition member (Liberal J. J. Blais) questioned Mike Wilson on the lost CANDU sales, he expressed concern over the "$2.8-billion loss" Canada had suffered. Answering the Blais question, Wilson told the Speaker: "I would like to correct the honourable member. The $2.8-billion figure is somewhat inaccurate. The total amount of exports at stake here as far as Canada is concerned was about $800 million. The balance was local costs in Argentina." Wilson seemed to have forgotten his own earlier statement on leaving Calgary, that, "If the contract is not signed now, $1.8-billion worth of business will be lost." So by his own calculation, even Mr. Wilson's Calgary figure had been 125 per cent too high. He was now stating that a new CANDU, started maybe a decade after the first one, would have cost *less* than the first Argentinian CANDU, which now had a price tag of $1.3 billion.

In response to further Question Period jabs Michael Wilson continued to deny that the Japanese turndown was a final position; questions about safeguards were turned aside; they would be dealt with next year by that parliamentary committee.

AECL, through the good offices of that finely tuned former Canadian diplomat, Ross Campbell (who had been our ambassador to NATO, where he'd also been bitter, complaining to the press about Trudeau government plans to reduce Canada's NATO military contributions — no dove, he), continued to flog CANDU reactors to Mexico, Yugoslavia, China, Indonesia, and South Korea. All resisted the golden-tongued AECL drummers for the remaining life of the Clark government, circa 1979.

There was a further, less obvious, long-term impact from the Argentinian turn-down and the Japanese freeze. Despite the fact that both disappointments had been building well before the Clark government was elected in May, those lost contracts hardened the views of many in the Tory caucus that the Red Tories, the "bleeding hearts" in their midst were bad for business. Thus Indira Gandhi, Japanese atom boss Iwazo Kaneko, and Argentina's Rear-Admiral Madero each in a different way contributed to Joe Clark's growing resolve. Only toughness, only good-for-business policies, only policies anti-thetic to all held dear by his Red Tories (he'd been called one himself, until now) would serve the cabinet, the party and, through them, the country.

Flora MacDonald's brief career as foreign minister in the 1979 Clark government more or less began and ended in Paris. Miss MacDonald arrived in Paris on June 12, just eight days after assuming her portfolio. She was met at the airport by Gerard Pelletier, the long-time friend and political ally of Pierre Trudeau (who had made him Canada's ambassador to France in 1976). Flora had ignored Roch LaSalle's demand that Pelletier resign and asked the former Quebec journalist to stay in his post. He agreed: "I see no reason to resign . . . I came to Paris to support a policy . . . not a party."

The new External Affairs boss, joined in Paris by John Crosbie, kept a low profile during the June meetings of the OECD. She spoke for continuing aid to developing nations but cautioned that such programs needed public support at home. Maybe warned by her companion that things were looking tough, she told a reporter after her maiden speech in an international forum that aid "must be weighed against domestic considerations." (In October John Crosbie went to meetings of world finance ministers in Malta and of the International Monetary Fund in Belgrade, Yugoslavia. At both meetings he warned that "easier loans" to developing countries with spiralling deficits made little sense; and he added that, in Canada, "our obligation is to our own people — the people who elected us. The developing countries have got to realize that we are simply not in a position to write a blank cheque.")

Then there was Tokyo the last week in June, and the economic summit meeting. Not much doing there, either. Joe Clark once again revealed his profound gift for small talk when, on arrival in Japan, he observed in his short statement at the airport that "It's obviously a very significant period for Japan."

Even though the Japan conference was to be chiefly concerned with oil prices and energy conservation, Energy Minister Ray Hnatyshyn was left in Ottawa. He whiled away the week worrying about how Canada would meet the modest conference commitments to reduce energy consumption, and complaining to reporters about his hemorrhoids, which he said had gotten worse since he'd joined the cabinet. A good deal of boundary-crossing between cabinet ministers obviously continued to mark the Clark cabinet style. It was External Affairs Minister MacDonald, who told reporters as she de-planed in Japan that Canada must begin considering and preparing for the prospects of restrictive speed limits, gasoline rationing, and higher oil prices. (Hnatyshyn's power base in the cabinet began behaving like an ice cube in a hot cup of coffee about as soon as he found his new office. Not only was Flora MacDonald discussing energy matters in Japan, the Prime Minister took over energy price negotiations with Alberta Premier Peter Lougheed; Michael Wilson was to be given responsibility for PetroCan; and an Ottawa reporter sent the Energy Minister a tube of Preparation H.)

At the headquarters of External Affairs in Ottawa, there was a heightened caution about talking out of school. Senior officials were pretty sure the new government, and the new minister, wanted to work changes in Canadian foreign policy, but they never quite figured out what those changes might be. What gave some of the young people in the department great delight, and many of the old timers great discomfort, was the change in *style*. They had not realized that Flora MacDonald was determined to make external affairs *interesting*. Speaking out on human rights at the U.N. and in Geneva as well as in Ottawa, Flora took to the world stage, after her timid beginning in Paris, with a zest unmatched by anyone in her protocol-bound job in Canadian history. Her critics said she was running for the Prime Minister's job, and remembered that both Louis St. Laurent and Mike Pearson had moved from External to 24 Sussex Drive. Her supporters said she was letting in some fresh air, making foreign relations and foreign aid rational and respectable by involving the Canadian people in her feelings and her views.

Power-tripper, egalitarian, or a bit of each? Probably not even Flora knew for certain. But no one who thought much about it (senior external mandarins excepted) could dislike the notion of encouraging the electorate to take a genuine interest in the country's foreign affairs. As the chatelaine of a worldwide staff of over 5,000, with an annual budget of $300 million plus (and another $1.2 billion to dispense through CIDA), Flora was indisputably doing things that mattered a lot — or at least overseeing them. No brilliant or startling policy initiatives emerged during the First Flora Dynasty; but the department did have a crystal-cut, diamond-bright persona. Flora's gutsy (sometimes nearly demogogic) speeches, her regal carriage, and her calculated flair for style of phrase and dress combined with her 1,000-candle-power smile to make her the brightest star in the Joe Clark firmament.

Other cabinet ministers who might have rivalled Mac-Donald's seamless public charisma appeared to lack the will, or the time. John Crosbie, for all his demonic energy and engaging manner, often looked like a man not sure he'd come to the right address. Maybe the party he'd wanted was somewhere down the block. He had also developed a fearful sense of mortality after a brush with a cerebral stroke a few years before.

David Crombie, already one of the best counterpunchers in the new Parliament, had a first-class mind, a vein of unalloyed toughness under a relentlessly cherubic exterior, and a genius for winning loyalty and genuine devotion from his supporters. He had youth and a charm that could bring birds out of their trees — or distract the most hardened bureaucrats from their flow charts; but he seemed to be in neutral, almost idling, or at least running below speed. (In

December, Parliament aborted, he spent Christmas in the intensive care ward of Toronto General Hospital, felled by a "minor heart attack").

The other David (and the other MacDonald) had personality to burn, too; but for him the intricacies of the Secretariat of State and the Ministry of Communications seemed wholly absorbing, perhaps even a bit intimidating, during those early months. Overworked in his dual cabinet functions (inner and outer), David MacDonald was a deliberate no-show in public.

So while Joe Clark worked fitfully at giving his cabinet an image described at its best as porous, Flora had the glitter of the centre ring much to herself. There were no miracles there, but no obvious pratfalls, either; and while some other cabinet colleagues were still being identified, discreetly, from the newspaper rogues' gallery scotch-taped inside commissionaire's booths on Parliament Hill, the External Affairs Minister was getting full delivery of every letter addressed simply "Flora, Ottawa."

A conscious student of Canadian political history, Joe Clark was well aware that until 1946 Canada had no ministers of External Affairs; foreign policy, until then, had been the Prime Minister's personal responsibility. Joe had a few swings at foreign policy, too. (His first, before the election, had been Jerusalem. None later was to hurt Clark, or embarrass Flora, quite so much.) At the Commonwealth Conference in Lusaka, Zambia, Canada's First Minister was not among the four keynote speakers; Australia's Prime Minister Malcolm Fraser got that nod. But Joe had one brief if diffident shot at glory. He suggested a five-point solution to the Rhodesian mare's nest: Ian Smith would have to leave the Rhodesian government, said Clark; the white minority would have to give up its special powers; the Patriotic Front would have to be involved in a settlement; the war would have to be ended; and a majority of the country's citizens would have to approve any settlement plan. It all sounded like a product of the same fertile mind that had noted "a very significant period for Japan."

Canadian newspapers reported that Clark had tried his plan out on British Prime Minister Margaret Thatcher. Mrs. Thatcher, always a lady, and a politician, "did not disagree with any of the points," according to "a Canadian official" who, as it turned out, worked in the PMO. The *Globe* story added that "she has not, however, committed herself to anything."

Canada did not press its plan to save Zimbabwe–Rhodesia. When, on Sunday, August 5, the conference leaders were preparing the Commonwealth ministers' position paper on Rhodesia, Joe and Maureen were sightseeing at Victoria Falls. Aussie P.M. Fraser had agreed to represent Canada's position at the final meeting.

This first-ever visit by a Canadian Prime Minister to Africa included stops in Cameroon (before the conference) and in Tanzania and Kenya (afterwards). To balance the visits to the pair of anglophone Commonwealth neighbours (the last two), the stay in Cameroon was stretched to three days, equalling the total in both other countries. On his arrival in Cameroon, Joe was treated to a 21-gun salute and greeted by a spontaneous demonstration from somewhere near 200,000 locals who had spontaneously equipped themselves with small, paper, maple leaf flags and postcard-sized photos of the Canadian visitor. Clark was asked to spontaneously increase Canadian foreign aid to Cameroon; he said no.

In Tanzania, Maureen and Joe saw a fertility dance; but reporters, who'd arrived early, later told their readers that the bare-breasted dancers had been covered after their rehearsals to avoid inflaming the passions of the prime ministerial party. President Julius Nyerere, unmindful of wildlife protection lobbyists in Canada, gave Joe a zebra hide; Maureen collected a leopard skin handbag.

Flying to Lahr, Germany, from Africa en route home, Clark joined reporters in the main cabin of the 707 to sing some boisterous French Canadian songs. (Many of them hadn't seen much of him until then; there'd been only two mini-buses to transport the press at the Lusaka conference, and one of them had broken down.) "I do feel good about this trip," the P.M. told the media on the flight; "Now all I have to do is not get stabbed by a bayonet when I inspect the troops in Lahr and then I'll be home free."

The highest marks scored for external policy during the seven-month Clark government came when, on July 18, Flora MacDonald and Immigration Minister Ron Atkey jointly announced Canada's willingness to accept "up to 50,000 refugees" from among the boat people fleeing Vietnam. The government program would be implemented on a "matching basis," they said. True to Flora's notion that the public should be involved in such policies, the government agreed to sponsor one refugee for every one sponsored by a private individual or group. There was a broad and generous public response to the policy. Not so, however, among many members of the Tory caucus who didn't think Canada ought to be importing refugees wholesale when we had over 7 per cent unemployment. Thus, by early December the plan worked out among MacDonald, Atkey, and Joe Clark had been scaled down some; now, it turned out, about 35,000 of that potential 50,000 people seeking sanctuary would have to be flown to Canada and supported during their period of transition by private guarantees and funds. The government, over the projected eighteen-month span of the scheme, would only sponsor 15,000 — not half of all the refugees, but rather less than half of those privately sponsored.

There were a few more miscues in the area of foreign affairs, but none to match the Jerusalem affair. At the beginning of September Agriculture Minister John Wise opened a week-long meeting of the World Food Council in Ottawa. At the meeting Mr. Wise won instant praise for a promise to provide new international food aid. He had the specifics:

Canada would add 110,000 metric tons of grain to the 490,000 tons already pledged to the new Food Aid Convention for the hungry of the world. Beyond that, Canada was going to set up a special new $2-million fund to help Third World nations develop strategies for agricultural development; and there was more — another $5.5 million more — a gift to the International Emergency Food Reserve, the organization on stand by for rush aid when food stores and crops were destroyed by disaster. The delegates were delighted. Mr. Wise got an ovation.

Then Joe Clark spoke to the meeting. Canada, said the P.M., unhappily had no new money at its disposal for any form of food aid. However the available funds were shuffled, the total could not be increased. After all, said Joe, Canadians "face the difficult but not intractable problems of inflation, unemployment, and erratic growth." As with parliamentary votes, applause may be regretted, but not retracted.

On December 3, the confusion in the Tory backfield was, again, between the Prime Minister and the Secretary of State for External Affairs. Pierre Trudeau was pressing the First Minister to explain what Canada was doing to bring pressure on the government of Iran to release the American hostages it held. Clark told the House: "We as the government of Canada have taken a role of leadership, through a variety of the forums open to us, that we believe will have influence on the Iranians."

Pressed as to specifics, and asked if Canada was considering trade sanctions against Iran, the P.M. responded: "Mr. Speaker, we are, naturally, considering whether sanctions by Canada, by the United States or by anyone else would be effective."

The newspaper headlines said: "P.M. hints at Iran Sanctions." But the body of the story noted an "explanation" given outside the House by Flora MacDonald. Trade sanctions against Iran were "only one option," said Flora. She thought "there was little chance the government would pursue" such a course given that there was "not much in the way of economic sanctions open to Canada," which did not, in fact, have much trade with Iran. Even the 2 to 5 per cent of Canada's oil consumption which originated in Iran came from the international inventories of the multinational oil companies, not directly from Iran to Canada. Canada would have some difficulty asking Exxon or Gulf to strain out the Iranian oil from any trans-shipped to Canada.

Joe Clark's biggest personal disappointment, his chance to be a statesman without going abroad, also foundered on the Iranian reef. On Thursday, November 8, at 5 P.M., U.S. President Carter suddenly cancelled the two-day visit to Ottawa which was to have begun just sixteen hours later. The hostage-holding in Iran was blamed for the last-minute cancellation. Plans for the visit had included a state dinner, which had to be called off, and a gala ballet performance at the National Arts Centre. Maureen McTeer's aides had to call twenty-four Canadian women to cancel a special coffee party. This was the fourth call each had received concerning the event. Initially the invitations had gone out to twenty-four of Canada's "leading women," to luncheon with Maureen and Mrs. Carter. But the U.S. First Lady had opted for a trip to visit Cambodian refugees over the Ottawa junket, so the invitations had been withdrawn, with regrets all around. Then, informed that President Carter's mother, Lillian, was coming, a new round of calls was made, announcing a coffee get-together instead; the last set of by now almost muttered calls was to call off the coffee-cup brigade as well. At least one event did not have to be rescheduled. The P.M.'s staff had declined the suggestion of the U.S. Chief Executive's brigade of advance men that Remembrance Day be moved up one notch on the calendar so Jimmy could lay a wreath on November 10. The regular ceremonies were able to proceed as planned.

On reflection, some of Clark's cabinet and advisors were as happy the talks had failed to occur. American officials had been planning some very heavy-handed "invitations" for Canada to provide much higher natural gas exports to the United States. Canada already had all the difficulty the cabinet needed with the energy debate for one year; any postponement was welcome. The Americans were poker players and their cards were high: Canada needed U.S. cooperation to build a gas pipeline to get the energy source out of the Arctic and the Americans knew it. The "quo pro" was going to be a very tough "quid" to chew whenever it was offered.

On December 10, Flora MacDonald was back in Paris, scene of her "coming out" as Foreign Minister. This time she was the guest for two days of French Foreign Affairs Minister Jean-François Poncet before going on to the NATO meetings in Brussels on December 12, the day John Crosbie would read his budget speech. While in Paris, *la belle* MacDonald talked to reporters about domestic politics; it seemed the Tory policy of "benign neglect" of Quebec was about to soften. Miss MacDonald said Ottawa would be intensifying contacts with Quebec City in the months leading up to the province's referendum on sovereignty/association in an effort to make the benefits of Confederation more apparent. But Parliament fell apart before Flora could tell Premier Lévesque about the advantages of hanging together.

At the end of the 1979 Clark World Series, the score charts showed no home runs; there had been a few clean infield hits (mostly from the team's travelling manager, MacDonald) but there had been some balks (the boat people; the John Wise food promises) and the spectators leaving the stadium mostly remembered that one disastrous error on the Jerusalem double-play. A lot wondered why shortstop Atkey hadn't been benched when Stanfield came out of retirement to hit the sacrifice bunt. Finally, despite MacDonald's crowd-pleasing, showboat tactics, it had been an inconclusive contest — and a dull game, from any vantage point.

~ 7 ~

The Provinces:
The Community of Communities

A foolish consistency is the hobgoblin of little minds,
adored by little statesmen. . . . With consistency a great
soul has simply nothing to do. Speak what you think
today in words as hard as cannon-balls, and tomorrow
speak what tomorrow thinks in hard words again,
though it contradict everything you say today.
—Ralph Waldo Emerson, "Essay on Self-reliance"

Judged by the Emersonian formula, Joe Clark was not in
1979 a man of "little mind." (His greatness of soul will be for
history to judge.) Particularly in dealing with Canada's
provinces the P.M. seemed to have taken a leaf from Emerson's
essay. His words may not have had the impact of cannon-balls
(the seeker-after-collegiality wanted consensus too much to
wound when a stroke would suffice), but they did seem to
have the momentum. Sometimes even after his intentions
had changed and the reversals been initiated, the impetus of

the Prime Minister's rhetoric evidently kept him careening along, missing his own turn in logic and will. He was, at such times, a bit like an out-of-control puppy on a highly waxed floor. He knew he wanted to be *over there* but here he was, still sliding precipitously towards a bad bruise on that door he'd already closed.

For example, in the dying days of the Trudeau govern-ment of 1974/79, in the 1979 spring election campaign, and over the summer and in speeches in Parliament (after it met in October), Joe Clark never tired of restating his view that it wasn't time yet to rebuild Canada's Constitution. That could wait. There'd been enough of the politics of confrontation, especially between Pierre Trudeau and René Lévesque. Now it was time for conciliation. What the people of Quebec were looking for, Clark told the House on November 2, 1979, was "not an exercise in salesmanship; they are looking for an exercise in reform."

And the new Tory government intended to give Quebec reform via the gift of federal powers and more adequate con-sultation. What the new government was not going to do, Clark emphasized time and again, was follow the Trudeau model of obsessively seeking to redraft the Constitution. No more constitutional conferences with Canada's provincial premiers were planned, and there was no master blueprint for constitutional overhaul hidden away in the PMO. Deeds were wanted now. There'd been enough of the Sun King approach to federal–provincial relations; the time was past for philosophical discourse. It would be pragmatic acts ini-tiated by Ottawa that would demonstrate confidence in the federal system and spread that confidence through the land. Grand design, in the pithy view of one Ontario Tory back-bencher, "is balls." Joe Clark obviously agreed.

Pressed in the House of Commons to proceed with the series of constitutional conferences begun under Pierre Trudeau, Clark said he wasn't going to do that. A new Constitution wasn't the answer. Instead, the P.M. told the House (on November 2, 1979):

> Our government will continue to make concrete proposals [that] . . . show . . . the federal government . . . can, in co-operation with all provinces, which it considers as partners and certainly not as enemies, demonstrate the possibility of a renewed federalism. . . . We began as soon as we became the Government of Canada, to make constitutional changes in the status quo in the country and, indeed, to make changes the previous government refused to make. I have no intention of convening a federal–provincial conference on constitutional matters quickly.

That was the system: step-by-step changes in federal–provincial relations, not lofty schemes to reshape the world. So, on November 5, pressed again on his plans in the House, Clark responded:

> There is no plan as such for changing our constitution. There is no grand design for constitutional reform.

And again, on November 8:

> As I have often indicated to the House and the rest of Canada, Mr. Speaker, our government's position concerning a renewed federalism is well known. . . . Mr. Speaker, it is my intention to carry on the process that we have already started, as a new government, by showing through concrete action that we are bringing specific changes in the federal government approach to constitutional matters.

The party line had also been spread to Quebec where

Clark's Minister of Federal–Provincial Relations William Jarvis, in an interview with the French daily newspaper *Le Devoir*, had said:

> A change of direction was needed, and our government has provided it. . . . If I had to use a single word to contrast our general approach . . . I would say that it is a pragmatic rather than a theoretical one. . . . There might be . . . cases where the constitutional provisions . . . will not be capable of accommodating to the new allocation of responsibilities considered . . . more appropriate. . . . The practice of federalism will then require that the Constitution be changed; and the government will not hesitate to change it. . . . As far as I know, Mr. Clark never excluded the possibility that it might be necessary to change the Constitution. . . . *What he did exclude is . . . a set of proposals aiming at a comprehensive renewal of the Constitution.*

So. All abundantly clear: it was to be reform, not salesmanship; and concrete proposals, but not grand design; Clark would give Canadians pragmatic, not theoretical change. But no "comprehensive renewal of the constitution." Right? Wrong.

Because in October, before all of those quotes were tucked into the pristine pages of Hansard, Joe Clark had confidentially commissioned a Quebec Senator Arthur Tremblay to study an overall review of —can you guess? —Canada's Constitution.

Adamant in his refusal in Parliament to bow to Liberal demands for a new set of federal–provincial constitutional talks, Clark had already changed his mind weeks before he brushed those requests aside. The day the Prime Minister told Parliament, and the rest of Canada via live T.V. coverage of the House, that: "There is no plan as such for changing our Constitution. There is no grand design for constitutional reform," that same day, Senator Tremblay was already at work on the mission he'd accepted the previous month.

No one outside the cabinet and the PMO knows for how many weeks or months before the Senator was phoned by the P.M. the actual decision to launch a new "grand design" had been made; it would have taken some time to make the determination and then to discuss the various candidates to head such a task force. They had to be familiar with federal–provincial relations and the current provisions of the British North America Act, Canada's Constitution (Arthur Tremblay was a former deputy cabinet minister in Quebec where he'd had charge of "intergovernmental affairs"). The candidates would ideally be drawn from Quebec in the hope that their report would be more palatable in that province; and they must be from the ranks of loyal Tory servants who could be trusted not to leak the fact they were working on a project the Prime Minister was busy ridiculing in the House of Commons.

That last requirement was critical. The person assigned to the study would be given a year to finish. By the time the report was made public no one would remember the P.M.'s denial of interest in any such policy; Canadian voters have a notoriously short attention span. But in the autumn of 1980, *after* the Quebec sovereignty/association referendum, the timing would be perfect. Joe Clark then would be able to meet Parliament in the fall, announce that he was calling a new constitutional conference, and present that conference with the Clark Manifesto for Renewed Federalism to end Quebec's grievances once and forever. But that would not happen until the fall of 1980; Canada's youthful Prime Minister had no interest in adding to his image as the U-turn king at this point in time. Besides, the Tory caucus had wall-to-wall members from small-town Ontario and the prairies who were wildly unenthusiastic about more concessions for Quebec and equally short on hunger for any more theory. Just as well to avoid force-feeding them a hefty dose of constitutional philosophy this year.

Canada's Tory Party has an unenviable reputation for eating its young and casting its old adrift. Joe could still remember his first meeting with the party's Ottawa caucus after his 1976 election as party leader. Only one M.P. had worked for his victory. He began his remarks that day with the courageous words: "I don't think I have many friends in this room." And he was right. Many of the M.P.s and party faithful hadn't even been sure young Joe was a Tory; some were still unsure in late 1979. No need now to give them cause to accuse him of playing boy-statesman, trying to emulate the Trudeau role in an effort to make the history books. Timing was everything in politics. One Tory had virtually created Canada 112 years ago; if young Joe was going to be this century's John A. Macdonald, and recreate Confederation, it would have to be next year.

There was no question of Senator Arthur Tremblay's not cooperating after his elevation to the Red Chamber by Joe Clark. When the P.M. decided to amend his timetable in the days just before Christmas 1979, he said merely that some preliminary work was under way; and, if re-elected, said Joe Clark, he could promise his government would have a full package of proposals for revision of the Constitution ready for autumn. Contacted by reporters, Senator Tremblay acknowledged that the Prime Minister had asked him back in October to begin work. "We are working on all aspects of the question," he said. Beyond that, the good Senator maintained his vow of silence. He refused to disclose his terms of reference or even the size or identity of his staff (assuming his use of "we" was not in the royal tradition). The Prime Minister who had delighted and surprised the press and public alike with his concepts of "open government" had not a word to say either about Senator Tremblay's overhaul manual for Canada's most fundamental political instrument, nor was anything said about the Senator's terms of employment, his remuneration, or even about the size and source of the budget for the study.

The puppy had finally gotten a grip on that glazed floor and negotiated the U-turn; but he had a visibly bruised nose again.

Overall, it was easier by far to find inconsistencies in Clark's handling of federal–provincial relations through 1979 than to search out any shining points of fidelity to policy in the rhetorical Tory haystack.

A fair description of the Clark view on whether his government would conduct any negotiations aimed at letting Quebec opt out of Confederation might be "unequivocally fluid." On November 1, 1979, the P.Q. government in Quebec released the text of the question to be placed on the sovereignty/association referendum ballot the following spring. Next day the P.M. made it absolutely clear to Parliament that his government would not deal with a Quebec government that claimed to have a referendum mandate to negotiate the terms of their withdrawal from Canada:

> Mr. Speaker, I realize that since the Quebec government has now made its official position public, the situation is much clearer than before. We now have the government's official position. It is no longer simply a matter of a party's stance. *This is incompatible with the idea of Confederation and it is unacceptable to the government of Canada.*

At his press conference that same day he underlined the point. The *Toronto Star* ran a red banner headline that proclaimed: "We won't negotiate Canada's break-up: Clark." Clark had told the press conference: "We have no intention of discussing the basic position of the Quebec government because as I have said it is an unacceptable position." Not only that: "There is no legal means by which self-determination can be realized." (There was, that is, no provision in the British

North America Act for any province to leave Confederation. So for a province to acquire self-determination legally Canada's Constitution would have to be changed.)

Not that it mattered. Canada's Prime Minister had just stated to the press of Ottawa and reiterated in Parliament that "We have no intention of discussing the basic position . . . it is an unacceptable position." That was certainly consistent. Throughout the spring election campaign Joe Clark had insisted that Quebec simply could not vote itself out of Confederation. Period.

But at the November 2 press conference there was one other comment of interest from the P.M.: "Obviously, if there were a massive political determination, one would have to consider changing the law." Obviously? Did he really suggest that he would "consider changing the law" (the Canadian Constitution) to let Quebec leave Canada if there were "a massive political determination" (a high "yes" vote in the referendum)? What about the "unacceptable position"?

The Prime Minister was undaunted. His forthright equivocation went mostly unremarked.

Clark's overall stance on Quebec sprang directly from his own years as a party worker and backroom specialist; his conditioning and his reflexes had been built and honed in Tory war rooms and through 10,000 intra-party memos ("I've spent my life in meetings") not in the later, briefer experience in the House of Commons. His confidence and comfort lay in and with party tacticians not parliamentary specialists (as clearly shown by his choice of inner staff).

So Quebec. For openers the province was unattainable electorally in the short term. The Liberal lock on polling stations around the province was burglarproof and the wary Québécois would not open the door from the inside for a stranger. So Clark's strategy was to make a strength of that weakness:

—Campaign, vis-à-vis Quebec, from the high ground of

principle since you could only get your ears torn off anyway, down there on the battlefield below. Tell voters there'd been enough of "escalating conflict" between Ottawa and Quebec City.

—Promise pragmatic reforms in place of the chimera of constitutional change.

—Use French in Parliament at every opportunity, and make the cabinet do likewise (to get that precious T.V. airtime in Quebec), and have cabinet members and Tory M.P.s show the flag in the province at every opportunity.

—Send Flora to France on her first mission abroad: the French understand symbolism. Drive home tokens and hints with every cost-free policy change in your grasp.

—Accept the Liberal-commissioned Chouinard report recommending that French and English both be used as languages of communication by pilots in Quebec airspace.

—Disband the PMO task force appointed by Pierre Trudeau to study and respond to every P.Q. government initiative; its head, Paul Tellier, could be transferred to Indian Affairs.

—Make it clear that civil servants were perfectly free, so long as they took no public party positions, to work in the Quebec referendum campaign in their own time. (There'd been enough trouble from them already in those two Ottawa seats in May; stay away from controversy there at all costs.)

—Kill the Liberal legislative plan to give the federal government power to hold nationwide referenda similar to Quebec's; describe the Liberal plan as "a veiled threat toward Canada's Québécois."

—Stay out of the referendum campaign. With only two elected M.P.s from the province (three, now, with that

Socred defection) and polls giving the Tories a humiliating 5 per cent of support in Quebec, it was a loser's
game.

—Build for the future, slowly and quietly. It was always
nice to be underestimated by your opponents; in two
elections or so there'd be time to strike at the gut for a
solid Quebec base; there was still time, lots of time, for
a Prime Minister who wasn't forty until the day after
he was sworn into office.

—Roll out the pork barrel and be certain those in Quebec
with influence to peddle were made aware it was open
for business.

—Appoint as Minister of Federal–Provincial Relations
someone "understanding." Bill Jarvis was ideal. Too
nice a guy to get in the Prime Minister's way — or to
resent Clark's assumption of most of his own respon-
sibilities — Jarvis also had the perfect mind-set: he was
a politician, not a theoretician or parliamentarian (his
whole political background, like Clark's, was as a party
organizer, campaign worker, fund raiser). He would
never intrude with rude (or worse, imaginative) policy
initiatives; in seven years in the House Jarvis had not
once mentioned constitutional or federal–provincial
affairs which he told a reporter he found a "bit esoteric."

On December 2, Joe Clark made certain Quebeckers
were informed the Tories were accepting applications for
patronage. The P.M. took a squad of his people to show-the-
flag at the Quebec P.C. Party annual meeting in Quebec City
— eleven cabinet members and fifteen M.P.s as well as four
senators. Speaking in relaxed French he introduced cabinet
colleagues "with excellent French names: Don Mazankowski,
Steve Paproski, Ramon Hnatyshyn," and "the Minister of
Finance who speaks neither French nor English; he comes
from Newfoundland." But no kidding about the new pro-
prietor of the Tory Quebec candy store; this was serious

© 1979. Reprinted with permission of the *Toronto Star* Syndicate.

business, meant seriously.

"Roch [LaSalle] is responsible for our purchasing policy," the P.M. explained. "Our purchasing surpasses $2.5 billion. That is not easy and it takes a good manager. Roch, you know, is also our political manager here, and that, too, is important."

The raunchy Minister of Supplies and Services beamed. The point was made and underlined. Happy days were here again.

It wasn't that Clark and his key advisors held les Québécois in particularly low esteem; it was the francophone members of the party — many of them battle-scarred veterans of many a provincial campaign for the Union Nationale —

who insisted that patronage and plenty of it was the only lever with which they could move aside the wall the Grits had built around Quebec voters. "Look at reality," was their lament. "We have 11,000 party members in the whole of the province. *Les rouges* have 135,000. We must begin somewhere."

Why not? One especially brutal assessment of the workings of Clark's internal clock, one that even he may not have been conscious of, postulated that the Tory P.M. was settling in for the long haul and was prepared to go one giant step beyond even Diefenbaker's cynically pragmatic Quebec electoral policy of 1957. (That was the year Gordon Churchill, a key Diefenbaker supporter and campaign manager, had invented his version of "benign neglect." Make a token gesture toward Quebec, the strategy of that year went, but otherwise ignore them. Save the money and time for seats we can win; then, next time around, the bastards will be crawling over each other to get on the bandwagon. And it *did* work. Diefenbaker won and formed a minority government virtually without Quebec representation in 1957 and went on to sweep large sections of the province in the 1958 reprise.) Now, with the P.Q. referendum in the offing, the ground rules were different. But an even more cynical strategy was now thinkable: let them opt out; it'll always be Liberal turf anyway. So negotiate them out of Confederation, and the Grits will go with them. We'll have it all. The Liberals have no enduring power base without Quebec so let's gerrymander the whole damn province right out of Parliament. When they discover it's not working — a few years down the road — they'll come begging to get back in and we'll take 'em back on our terms. By then we'll have the lock the Grits have always had until now.

But that was long term — and, in fairness, apocryphal. What mattered here and now was the need to make simple points abundantly clear to Quebec party workers (first) and Quebec voters (later). Les Québécois would soon understand Conservative policy toward Quebec even if it remained enigmatic to *les maudits anglais.* It really didn't matter if English Canadians understood Tory Quebec policy so long as they weren't afraid of it. Clark *had* tried to frighten everybody of the Liberal position of confrontation with Lévesque which, in a rather alarming flight of logic, he said, "helped elect a bunch of Liberal members to Parliament," while at the same time it had somehow "helped to elect a Parti Québécois government and . . . helped to create a very strong constituency for separatism."

Joe Clark's other breath-taking gallop to a conclusion was that it would be wrong for him to campaign against the P.Q. referendum not only because he wasn't "a resident of Quebec" but because it "would be interpreted as an interference in the referendum question in the province of Quebec."

If Clark's Quebec policy was blurred by a haze from those smoky backrooms, his overall approach to the country as a whole had never been in doubt. Born in the post-patriotic era after Expo '67, Clark's federalism seemed to owe little to a sense of national destiny or community. (Ed Broadbent had described it as a philosophy that saw Canada as being somehow less than the sum of its parts.) It was a homey, neighbourhood kind of philosophy; one geared to folk who liked to bash Ottawa and build bigger lily pads in smaller ponds; and it perfectly expressed the Clark view that every man's region or province is his castle, linked, it seemed, only tenuously to the rest of Canada.

But his philosophy was clear. From the beginnings of the 1979 election the Tory leader had been foursquare behind his doctrine that Canada was "a community of communities." It was his campaign rallying cry, his credo and catechism, his gut perception of the nature of Canada. It was to be reinforced serially through the summer and fall as Joe found federal goodies to turn over to the provinces. There'd been too much centralization; it was time the provinces were given resources adequate to their needs. Then alienation would cease, and only the sounds of murmuring mutual affection would be heard throughout the land. There were literally hundreds of occasions to fly the banners of decentralization and flog the wicked Liberals who wanted to keep the provinces as suppli- cants at the groaning federal banquet table. Subsequent to the spring pledges to "make the provinces full partners in confederation [by] . . . strengthening our community of communities," Clark continued to emphasize his stance.

For example, on September 14, speaking to reporters in Halifax, Joe Clark said Canada's regions "are going to become strong only if they have cards of their own to bring to the federal–provincial table." Then on October 10, in Parliament, he announced: "The extent to which all provinces have the economic means to exercise their powers will determine their ability to pursue their different cultural, social, and economic goals. . . . The greater their dependence on Ottawa for their revenues, the less likely they are to develop that diversity which is at the heart of the Canadian ideal." And more, in Parliament: "The test of our federalism and its strength is not in the undoubted power of the central government to have its way."

That was October, in Ottawa. Now to Spruce Grove, Alberta. You remember Spruce Grove and the Spruce Grove Arena? That's where the grinning new Prime Minister-elect had promised on May 22 to introduce the measures to build his "renewed federalism" and his "community of communi- ties" as soon as he took office; the place where the whole process of housebreaking the mad dog centralists of Ottawa was set in motion just hours after the polls closed.

So to Spruce Grove again. But now the date is December 19, 1979; same fellow though: "We must face the fact that the federal government is not as able as it should be to manage the national economy . . . and to conduct major national policies."

And there was more, from the High River gent who had

wanted the provinces to come to table in Ottawa with their own cards. Joe went on to quote from the text of the Economic Council of Canada, which had published a study of federal–provincial relations sometime earlier. The P.M. read the words of the Economic Council report with full approval and blessing: Unless fiscal relations between the federal and provincial governments were re-examined, and quickly, he read, *" 'the government's management of the economy will become increasingly powerless to the perils of the country as a whole and the welfare of every Canadian.'"* The apostle of decentralization was saying that he needed to have some of those powers back in Ottawa.

He had a proposal, too. Mr. Clark thought the federal government should commission a new study of federal–provincial relations. After the election it would do so either alone or in concert with the provinces, said the P.M.; and the report would be ready well before the current federal–provincial cost-and-revenue-sharing deal expired in 1982 and had to be renegotiated.

Just days before, in the wake of the Clark government's agreement to pass a series of powers to the provinces in the period between May and December, the Economic Council report was being widely used by editorial writers and opposition critics to whip the Prime Minister. He was now an unabashed convert and, like all such, an even truer believer than his new group of economic gurus.

So what about the community of communities? Let the Prime Minister add just this about that: "Without the ability to implement national economic policies, Canada's economy could be fragmented and vulnerable."

Joe Clark had retraced his own steps to Spruce Grove in more than a literal sense. But in the interval between May 22, and December 19, 1979, the P.M. had already managed to give, or promise, some very substantial powers back to the provinces.

One of the biggest presents was to be Loto Canada. In

1978 Ottawa had cleared a profit of $74 million from the sale of the federal lottery tickets. In the spring campaign, Clark had said that Ottawa would get out of Loto Canada if he were elected. "We don't need two levels of government in the lottery field," said Clark then. After a little foot-dragging, Alberta M.P. Steve Paproski, Clark's Minister of Fitness and Amateur Sport, convened a conference of the provincial ministers in charge of lotteries in Ottawa on August 21. Later, on September 25, Paproski announced the provinces would pick up the tab for an $18-million hockey arena program the previous Liberal government had promised to finance from Loto Canada funds. The provinces would also pay Ottawa a $24-million annual share of Loto Canada proceeds; and the name would stay the same (leaving ticket buyers, maybe, to go on believing all those wonderful chances to win a tax-free million were showered on them by Paproski the philanthropist). But, those conditions met, Ottawa was going to stop running lotteries. Joe's campaign promise had been made good and Ottawa had given away at least $50 million annually of the economic muscle the P.M. wanted so badly to flex in December. Said Steve Paproski, announcing the Ottawa giveaway in September: "This agreement heralds a new era in federal–provincial relations."

The really huge potential Ottawa gift to the provinces though came at the beginning of September when the P.M. announced after a ninety-minute Ottawa meeting with Newfoundland Premier Brian Peckford that the federal government was going to give the province control over offshore mineral rights. Joe Clark had promised the rights to Peckford, a Tory premier who'd worked for the Clark victory, back in May, and he was determined to keep his promise. Soon he'd make a similar announcement in Halifax, for the benefit of Nova Scotia's P.C. Premier John Buchanan. Clark also flew to Newfoundland where he was served a generous tot of screech for breakfast and told Peckford was still hungry — he now wanted full provincial rights over commercial fishing. The likely early beneficiaries of the new Clark largesse would be Newfoundland, Nova Scotia, and British Columbia, all of whom had been fighting Ottawa for years in a vain attempt to get what they'd now been promised without having had to raise a hand or retain a single constitutional lawyer. B.C.'s Socred Premier Bill Bennett had been given the freest ride of all; he'd not even campaigned for the Tories in 1979.

Unlike Loto Canada, however, the offshore rights couldn't be handed over with the stroke of a pen. It would take a constitutional amendment — one of those "pragmatic" as opposed to "theoretical" changes — and that could take three or four years. But a renewed Clark electoral mandate would probably seal the deal — or would it, after the announcement in Spruce Grove, circa December 1979?

One Clark minister, the tough-minded Sinclair Stevens, had actually tried to get some money *from* the provinces in 1979. As they were always asking for data from Ottawa, and asking that extra questions relevant to their needs be added to the Canada Census form, Stevens suggested they should pick up part of the $80-million tab for Canada's 1981 census. The provinces declined that offer.

Other things offered or given the provinces during the 1979 Clark regime concerned powers rather than money. For example Bill Jarvis told Parliament on October 25 that the government would follow through on plans to give the provinces full authority over laws governing marriage and divorce — raising the charming spectre of at least one province adopting very liberal divorce legislation, for example, and becoming the Reno-of-the-north with a crazy quilt of divorce and marriage regulations in various provinces. (Might not Niagara Falls lobby Ontario Premier William Davis, for example, for laws permitting instant marriage-on-demand to bolster the economy of the honeymoon capital?) The Stratford lawyer who'd been made Minister of Federal-Provincial

Relations told the House he was hoping the issue could be settled quickly.

Communications Minister David MacDonald announced at the end of November that he was now prepared to give the provinces half the T.V. loaf they'd been unable to wrest from the Liberals. MacDonald said he was going to arrange to transfer authority over cable television and pay T.V. to the provinces; Ottawa was even willing to share the controls over programming, said MacDonald. And the right to issue licences, always a prime field for those concerned with patronage, would be passed to the provincial governments.

Not everyone was surprised by Joe Clark's late realization that Ottawa had already shed an uncomfortable amount of the clout it needed to deal effectually with regional economic disparity. The total amount and percentage of tax revenue going to Ottawa, as compared with that going to the cities and provinces, had been dropping every year since the end of the Second World War. By 1961, the balance had shifted: Ottawa was getting less than half the taxes paid in Canada each year. By 1978, Canada's city and provincial government were spending six tax dollars for each four dollars spent by the feds. At the same time the amount of money being turned back to the provinces (and, through them, to the cities) was rising dramatically. In 1958, 5.6 per cent of Ottawa's money went to the provinces; by 1978 the figure was 22 per cent, a whopping 400 per cent increase.

Before Clark's election, back in 1978, national goals and priorities were already being affected by the shifting locus of power. When Pierre Trudeau was trying to sweeten the tempers of provincial premiers (whose support he wanted for his scheme of constitutional reform) he'd taken all the strings off federal money contributed to support provincial health insurance schemes. Soon after, doctors began opting out of the plans, and the federal government was helpless to maintain the universal service it had originally promised Canadian voters. Quebec demands over the years for unconditional, no-strings grants from Ottawa developed a snowball effect; unwilling to make special rules for one province, Ottawa had offered all provinces similar opting-out privileges or rights to take lump-sum grants and distribute them as they saw fit. Many provinces had followed the Quebec lead.

So by the time Joe Clark rushed to jam his fingers into the dikes protecting provincial rights in 1979, the holes had mostly already been plugged and the threatening federal tides of centralization had long since dissipated. All Joe got for his trouble (as he finally realized in December) was a set of bruised fingers and a view of the mud flats outside the dike.

Nevertheless, Canadians had felt in 1979 that the Clark team would be able to solve problems that had proved intractable to Liberal fixes. Joe was, if nothing else at all, a Tory; and the premiers of seven Canadian provinces were of the same faith and persuasion. Joe never tired of proclaiming those friendships. But, as we saw earlier, such friendships are difficult to maintain when two of one's friends have different goals and needs.

In trying to stay friends with both Alberta's Peter Lougheed and Ontario's Bill Davis — the former chasing glory via rapidly escalating oil prices, and the latter struggling to maintain Ontario's industrial hegemony and, to that end, lower oil prices — the neophyte P.M. was bound to end up looking like a rookie cop who'd been assaulted by both husband and wife after trying to settle a domestic dispute. Clark had his M.A. in political science; but he seemed heedless of the historic lesson that the imperatives of power and survival have always had precedence over the flimsy friendships based on the casual coincidences of a shared party name or philosophy. The P.M.'s ingenuous confidence that he could perform the impossible, and at the same time stay friends with everybody, left observers with their mouths agape. It was a lot like watching a kiddy car hell bent on a collision course with a moving van, the car's youthful operator's vision obscured by a hedge and the siren songs of speed and power rendering him deaf to warning shouts.

Then there was the question of how close, firm, and fixed those friendships might have been anyhow. Peter Lougheed had never been accused of being a wholly uncritical admirer of the young fellow from High River who'd once worked as a Lougheed assistant. The Alberta premier had avoided running for the Tory federal leadership, which he could have won handily in 1976. It wasn't that he didn't want it, rather that the Lougheed group had decided the Conservative Party couldn't beat Pierre Trudeau, and Lougheed had no itch to be leader of the opposition. After the voting, Lougheed had been conspicuous by his absence when Joe Clark strode to victory across the frenetic Ottawa Civic Centre. When Pierre Trudeau self-destructed in 1979, giving Joe Clark a cakewalk to 24 Sussex Drive, Peter Lougheed was given the first major reason ever to doubt his own political acumen — and none to love Joe Clark. The Alberta boss knew too, whether Clark did or not, that they had to clash over oil policy and prices. With huge cash reserves accumulating from oil revenues in Alberta, the Lougheed government had already begun using their money-machine to pull the Canadian economic centre of gravity westward before Clark was elected; they had momentum going for them now and they weren't about to let go by making major concessions on oil price hikes.

Joe needed Alberta oil but he had a power imperative, too; there were ninety-five parliamentary seats in Ontario. So, with Quebec denied him as an electoral base, Clark would always opt for Davis over Lougheed in a two-way fight. It was, after all, those twelve Metro Toronto seats, part of the fifty-seven harvested in Ontario, that had made Joe Clark Prime Minister.

There was, however, some doubt about how far a Bill Davis alliance would extend in a crunch. Like the Alberta premier, Ontario's undisputed Tory czar had watched Joe Clark erase any lingering dreams he had of life at 24 Sussex Drive. Whether or not Davis had personally lusted for the pleasant trip from Queen's Park to Parliament Hill, many of those around him, aides, advisors, and cronies, had hankered for a turn on the larger stage; and they knew they'd get it only if Davis paid the entrance fee. They weren't grateful to the rather stiff and distant young man who'd denied them the chance. Moreover, they were uncomfortable with Clark and many of his people, who seemed to them to be a bit remote and too carefully programmed. Clark and his gang didn't sit well with the loose and often raucus bunch who poured (and sometimes poured and poured) through the Queen's Park Legislative Building in Toronto. Ontario Tories were still the provincial Bourbons, fat on thirty-six years of uninterrupted political rule; they were cocky and unswerving in their good-old-boy confidence in things to come, even after five years in minority government.

Appearances were maintained; at least most of them. Bill Davis was the first Clark dinner guest at 24 Sussex Drive on June 13, actually the day before the Clarks officially moved into the thirty-five-room residence. They were just three for dinner. Did Bill ask Maureen about her appearance in a Carleton School of Journalism film about the 1971 Ontario Tory leadership convention? Maureen had been a worker at that conclave for Bert Lawrence. When Bill Davis won the leadership Maureen told the film camera: "It seemed to have been such a good chance for a new wave, and it seems to have ended in such a little ripple." The Carleton student film caught Maureen explaining why she'd abstained when her candidate had failed to survive until the last ballot: "I was unable to bring myself to vote for what I believed was the dying establishment."

Now that "little ripple" of that "dying establishment" was a dinner guest of a still youthful Maureen McTeer in her role as wife and hostess of the Prime Minister of Canada. What *did* they talk about?

At another dinner five months later, Bill Davis took time to lecture young Joe on political realities before a 2,500-person banquet party who'd paid $150 a plate at a Toronto fund-raising dinner. "There is no question that one-and-one-half million Albertans must have their fair share," Davis allowed. "But," he added, looking at the Prime Minister, "you have the tough task of speaking for 22 million Canadians who also have their rights and expectations."

The accommodation hadn't been nearly so spacious ten days earlier when Davis had gone to Ottawa again at the head of Ontario's delegation to the one-day, November 12, federal–provincial conference on energy prices. Joe's office had telexed the Ontario government saying there'd be room at the conference table for only six advisers to the Ontario premier. (Davis took his usual constellation of twenty-five, and they all got in.) It was inevitable that Clark and Davis would go on crowding one another for their respective advantage.

It's curious that politicians are always the last to realize that other practitioners of their trade rarely reciprocate generosity. No Canadian government has ever wrested advantage in negotiations with the United States by giving away a few concessions to set the right tone for what was to follow. Nor has any Prime Minister ever won a single favour by first giving some or all of the provinces a little something on account. Cable T.V., Loto Canada, offshore fishing rights, and the rest had bought nothing for Joe Clark but the same learning experience he could have had from a five-dollar, paperback history of Canadian politics. The worst of it was that as Bill Davis, Peter Lougheed, and the others began to deliver their ritual compliments at public meetings, the Clark assurances that he "could do it better" began losing their grip on the public imagination. And he knew it.

But there was still Parliament. There, the P.M. was accorded the respect he so richly merited. And Joe Clark, as everybody knew and said, was first of all a parliamentary man. That was his natural constituency, a comfortable old shoe compared with the international crown of thorns or the federal-provincial hair shirt.

~ 8 ~

Clark's Parliament:
Government in Free Fall

Attempting to analyze the Clark government's record in
Parliament after its destruction is a bit like discussing the art
and technique of a sky-diver's period of free fall after it is clear
he jumped without a parachute. As with the sky-diver, the
definitive comment on the Tories in Parliament in late 1979
was fully stated by a damp spot on the carpet adjacent to the
Treasury Benches in the House. Events in the days leading up
to the December 13 climax of the 1979 Silly Season had not,
nonetheless, been without interest or irony though they'd
begun badly.

The Throne Speech carefully read by Governor General
Ed Schreyer on October 9 had been received by the country at
large (in a memorable Dalton Camp phrase, used to describe
an earlier speech by Joe Clark) "with a sitting ovation." After
requiring a longer post-election gestation than any other
Canadian government since Confederation, the Tory cabinet
finally summoned the parliamentary midwives only to be

delivered of a gnat — and one that was curiously shy and reluctant to speak of the life before it. The speech contained no description of a detailed energy policy, although Energy Minister Ray Hnatyshyn had throughout the summer promised a "dramatic and inspirational" blueprint "soon." More amazing: the Speech from the Throne made not the faintest mention in any of its words and parts of the province of Quebec — of the Parti Québécois referendum on sovereignty/association, of Canada's Constitution — or of any part of the globe outside Canada's borders. Neither Canada's most parlous domestic problem nor any matter at all of external affairs got so much as a nod, a nudge, or a wink. There were earnest intimations of the government's desire to learn more about the strange, new world it found itself in; the Clark regime indicated that it wished eight parliamentary committees to be appointed. The speech did (without mention of Quebec) pledge Joe's spirit-of-renewal in federal–provincial relations; more open government was promised along with freedom of information legislation, parliamentary reform, a system to give parliamentary committees more authority, and a clutch of "sunset laws" under which government corporations, boards, and the like would have to justify their continuance rather than doddering into the pension-lined sunset *sans* scrutiny.

Economy strategy got a good deal of attention both implied and explicit: Canada would achieve energy self-sufficiency by 1990 by means not explained; there would be more emphasis on individual initiative and (more apple pie) a reduction in the taxation burden on the taxpayers (Sinc Stevens bureaucracy-bashing?); the promised mortgage-interest-property-tax-credit scheme was present and accounted for as a way to help Canadians "build a stake in Canada." But there was no mention of the $2 billion in tax cuts Joe Clark had promised during the election — that "stimulative deficit" he'd advocated and said he would give Canadians while busying himself with budget balancing in his free time.

The High River lad had gotten off on the wrong foot with the Senate, having his staff appropriate some of the Red Chamber's coveted gallery guest seats for Clark cronies, while the wives of some members of the "other place" were left to shiver in the outer darkness for want of a place to plant their couturier-clad bottoms. (David Crombie, Clark's Minister of Health and Welfare, didn't get a seat, either; he watched the Throne Speech by clambering onto the base of a marble pillar which he clasped warmly to his vest to maintain his vantage and view during the reading.)

Born under the astrological sign of the twins, Clark's Throne Speech apparently signalled a turning away from the swash-and-buckle of ad hoc policy promises and a return to the other persona — the weaving shadow-boxer schooled in a hundred political campaigns where the chief trick was to present a moving target; keep the head well down between the shoulders was the rule; tuck in your chin was the advice; don't give 'em anything to hit. More than one observer looking in vain for the bone, meat, and gristle beneath the opaque parchment with which Parliament had begun its fatal journey was reminded of the Ontario premier of the early forties, Mitch Hepburn. Trying to get a grip on the policies of the Canadian Prime Minister of that day, Mackenzie King, was, said Hepburn, "like trying to nail jelly to the wall."

Brief, bland, and banal, the speech was barely longer than John Diefenbaker's first; but the prairie populist had filled his maiden thrust with specifics and innovative ideas; there were few of those this day; for once the members' wives' gowns really were more stimulating than the polished words dropping like confetti into the pool of listeners and leaving neither splash nor ripple behind.

Diefenbaker, missing his first Throne Speech since 1940, lay at rest now, if not at peace, in the quiet cemetery outside Prince Albert. The Chief's valedictory, mercifully unpublished before young Joe had to meet "his" Parliament for the first time, had been made to two denizens of the National Press Club in Ottawa August 15, just one day before his death. Diefenbaker had encountered the pair as they were leaving their headquarters; both were wearing black T-shirts, bearing the legend "Election '79," which had been distributed to its technical staff by the CBC the previous spring. John Diefenbaker asked what the T-shirts represented, and was answered. Never able to pass an opportunity combining the chance for a pun and a barb combined, the old man shook his head in mock despair: "Ah, yes. May 22. Well, that was the blackest day in Canada's history. You're right to wear them." The eighty-three-year-old ex-P.M. told them he was still planning to visit China but was having difficulty with his doctor, who wasn't sure the Diefenbaker heart could stand the necessary immunization shots for such a trip. He laughed, waved, and stepped briskly away toward his office and, within sixteen hours, his death. But his last day had included the elements he'd have wanted in it — a moment to yarn and reminisce and a final feel of the lance in his hand and the swift barb on his tongue.

The fine-grained clarity and focus of hindsight and reflection make it easy to ascribe reasons to the bloopers in the early days of Canada's twenty-first government which led in an exponential curve to the debacle of December 13. At the time there was just a feeling that things were slightly skewed, that the new hand on the tiller might not be firmly instructed by any particular sense of direction.

After the event the strongest impression is that Joe Clark lacked an empathy gland — that he failed to understand the limits beyond which men can't endure pushing — that he relied on backroom political logic while oblivious to the fact that duels have been fought to the death and dynasties toppled over imagined slights and casual insults. *Globe and Mail* columnist Geoffrey Stevens probably summed up best for the prosecution when he headed a piece in that paper with the pithy George Bernard Shaw quotation: "Reformers have the idea that change can be achieved by brute sanity." Shaw wasn't discussing Clark in Parliament and neither was Stevens; but both might have been.

An early auger presented itself the day after the Throne Speech (which is delivered in the Senate chamber as the Queen or her representative can enter the Commons only by special leave, thanks to Charles II). As the M.P.s assembled in their respective places in the House of Commons some noted that Metro Toronto's three cabinet ministers, Messrs. Crombie, Atkey, and Wilson (all by-passed in selections to Clark's inner cabinet) had suffered one more slight: all three were seated in the second row of government benches. The more prestigious and therefore preferred front benches had been awarded elsewhere. Not unfailingly trustful of the Bay Street fellows himself, Clark had many western and Maritime M.P.s with him who were openly rancorous towards any manifestations emanating from Fat Cat City, as one called it. Now that they'd clawed their way to the centre of power they were damned if it would be dominated from Toronto. But David Crombie, at least, was known to have some leverage with Premier William Davis of Ontario. And Clark's electoral victory had hung on those Metro Toronto seats — seats where Crombie's candidacy had lent great credibility to the Tory campaign, along with Bill Davis's Big Blue Party Machine; and Joe Clark would have to return to that same well to drink on another occasion.

Then there were the six Social Credit members. Here, as with the Metro Toronto members of cabinet, the P.M. had some internal problems in his caucus and party. House of Commons rules said any party having elected twelve or more members was entitled to "official recognition as a party." That mattered because officially recognized parties had very special perks denied to those members fuzzily identified only as independents or members of rump groups. Most visibly, any officially accepted party would be regularly "recognized" by the Speaker of the House, James Jerome. That meant the party's leader would be permitted to speak on every major issue before the House after leaders of other parties in order of their size; that in turn meant more press coverage, more opportunity to express the party line — or hammer the government line — and more of that priceless T.V. coverage. It would even mean more press interviews in the post-Parliament scrums: "Would you amplify/explain your remarks in the House this afternoon/evening?" There were other more tangible benefits. If accorded party status in the House, the Socred members would qualify for somewhere between $170,000 and $200,000 dollars in government subsidies for the employment of research staff and other facilities. By contrast, M.P.s lacking party status lacked even a caucus room to call their own.

In 1974 the Social Credit Party had elected eleven members, just one short of the regulatory requirement. Nonetheless, after consideration by an all-party committee, they had been given all the benefits offered other groups in the House. On June 7, 1979, Quebec Socred leader Fabien Roy told reporters in Ottawa he was confident his group would again be given full status although he added, after a meeting with the new Prime Minister, that the matter couldn't be formally settled until Parliament met in October.

M. Roy either hadn't listened in his conference with Joe Clark, or the P.M. had changed his mind; it didn't take until October. On June 17 — just ten days after a rosy parliamentary future had been sketched by M. Roy — an aide in the Prime Minister's office telephoned the Social Credit members to tell them the leader had decided they could not have party status, after all.

"He told us there was very strong pressure from the Conservative candidates defeated in Quebec, that there was a great reticence to give us any money," said a party spokesman. All true. Quebec Tories believed that the Social Credit party could be wiped out in the next election; it had already dropped from eleven seats to six and had been a waning, rural splinter group in visible decline ever since the death of Real Caouette, its charismatic leader of the sixties. If the Socreds could be totally eliminated, reasoned Quebec Conservatives, then any anti-Liberal vote, no longer split between them, would all accrue to Tory candidates.

The Clark government was going to need the Socred votes in the House to maintain a hair-thin majority on want-of-confidence motions if the Liberals and New Democrats ever found it in their hearts to bloc-vote. But, Clark was assured, the Social Credit M.P.s didn't have to be appeased as a group for that support. There were at least two other routes to Damascus:

1. The Social Credit members were as able to do their sums as the Quebec Tories; they didn't want a new election until there was no alternative left; they'd support the government simply because they didn't want to go home again. Even without party status, Ottawa and its perks were damned pleasant.

2. Some, maybe all, the Socred M.P.s could be "had." Most were clones of Tory M.P.s from eastern Ontario or the prairies — self-made auto dealers or dentists, small c Conservatives, hard liners on abortion and capital punishment — and they'd be perfectly at home in the Tory caucus. It would just take a little time. And the brass ring would be an assured parliamentary majority of three votes anyway and a clear, five-year run in power.

By the end of July there'd been a bit of fudging by a Joe Clark assistant, and a quick recovery by government House Leader Walter Baker. Clark's aide had said that the whole question of research grants for the Socreds was still open, and would be decided by "a committee." Not quite right, said a spokesman for Baker. The decision would be made by a "quasi-committee" called the Commissioners for Internal Economy; the committee's personnel would comprise Mr. Baker, Treasury Board President Sinclair Stevens, two other cabinet ministers, and the Speaker of the House — when that official was named.

The third weekend in September some of the private advice given Joe Clark started looking accurate. One of the Socred M.P.s, unilingual francophone Richard Janelle, bolted his party and joined the Prime Minister for an announcement he would henceforth sit in the government benches. There had been no price or promises exacted for the defection, said Clark. (And indeed Janelle had to wait several weeks for his appointment as a parliamentary secretary.)

Operating on a one-down-five-to-go philosophy, Roch LaSalle redoubled his efforts to attract more recruits from both Socred and Quebec Liberal ranks. With Janelle corralled, the government was just three members short of a one-vote majority in the House since the P.M. had reappointed Liberal M.P. James Jerome as Speaker. (A pair of Tory by-election losses later in the fall shrank the margin to just a one-vote majority *with* full Social Credit support.)

But by late September Joe Clark had to put LaSalle on a shorter leash. One Liberal M.P., Celine Hervieux-Payette, told reporters she'd been guaranteed a cabinet post if she'd switch parties. (Not a bad choice; she had both the qualities Joe Clark was trying to add to the government's public image: she was French and she was female.) But that story and a string of others like it persuaded the P.M. that the daily embarrassment in the press was outweighing the slim possibility of encouraging other switch-hitters so early in the game. He told Roch LaSalle to close the recruiting office.

Fabien Roy may have had the last laugh. On September 28 it was revealed he'd written R. H. Simmonds, Commissioner of the RCMP, asking for a full investigation of possible illegal activities by Progressive Conservatives who were the subject of "rumours that the M.P. for Lotbiniere [Janelle] was offered a post" to defect. Clark's Solicitor General Allan Lawrence felt obliged to reply that the charges were "some sort of public relations dodge by the Social Credit."

After appointment of Jerome as Speaker the "quasi-committee" inflicted the final humiliation: no Socred research funds. It would be okay, Joe Clark was constantly reassured; they were "only clowns" anyway and would not dare force an election. They'd hang in.

When the House met the Social Credit M.P.s began by proving the thesis. They supported the government every-time it needed help. But Fabien Roy, the Socred leader, was slowly working up the indignation that would eventually bring him and his party to abstain from voting December 13, sealing Parliament's fate.

On October 2, Roy warned that he and his colleagues could disrupt House proceedings if they weren't relieved of their non-person exile. On October 26, still being snubbed, they did just that. When Question Period began that day the Socred M.P.s resumed their heretofore fruitless quest for Speaker Jerome's eye and permission to speak. Foiled again by the protocol of party turn-taking, they began rising and speaking anyway, their voices mixing with those of the "recognized" questioners. After about ten minutes of being mostly ignored excepting by the Speaker, who kept repeating that if the "honourable members had a point of privilege" they could raise it at the end of Question Period, Fabien Roy tried making a point-of-order and was instantly overruled by Jerome. All five M.P.s then left their seats, bowed to the Speaker in traditional fashion, and walked out of the House. "We'll keep on doing it until they realize that we have rights here," said Roy to reporters outside the House.

Government House Leader Walter Baker said the next day that the Speaker would have "no alternative" but to eject them if the Socreds repeated their behaviour. But that wasn't necessary; the M.P.s didn't get party status, but they did start catching the Speaker's eye quite regularly. It wasn't until a week later that the Speaker and Walter Baker were both forced to deny Liberal charges in the House that a deal had been struck to buy the continuing support of the Social Crediters. In a lengthy and rancorous debate Baker conceded that he had been "moved" by the expression of outrage on the face of one Social Credit M.P. leaving the House and had spoken to James Jerome to see whether the Socreds could perhaps have more time in Question Period. Speaker Jerome agreed with opposition spokesmen that it would have been quite improper for the government House Leader to have made any "representations" on the matter; but Baker hadn't made a representation, said Jerome, merely "a suggestion." Whatever. It took.

After the Crosbie budget was introduced, the Social Crediters made a last, despairing effort to serve their constituents and to use the balance of power that they'd supposed they had in the minority House. They demanded the government withdraw the proposed eighteen-cent hike in gasoline tax which they said would be unbearable for the low- and middle-income families who were their constituents. A back-off by the government would permit them to sustain the Tories in the want-of-confidence motion to come; without the concession, they said, they would abstain from the vote. The Clark strategists couldn't back down that far after all the fine rhetoric Crosbie had given the House about the need for fiscal restraint, belt-tightening, and moving gas and oil prices closer to the world norms.

The Conservatives refused to give the Socreds their concession, but Fabien Roy claimed he was offered an alternate deal just fifteen minutes before the government fell on a recorded vote. The budget had also included a tax credit to offset the rising fuel costs for low income families. Roy told reporters he was approached by a Clark emissary in the

House and told the government would pledge to double that tax credit (at a cost to the taxpayers of $1 billion) if Roy's group would stay in the House and vote with the government. Roy said he'd refused to accept the billion-dollar Tory bid to stay in power because it had come "too late to accept it in honour," even though it would have relieved the burden on his constituents.

Outside the House, John Crosbie said there had been such a deal proposed, but that it had been initiated by the Social Crediters, not by the Tories. "That's not the way we play the game," added the Finance Minister.

Said Roy: "Clark was too proud to come to me earlier. It wasn't up to me to go to him. After all, it was his budget."

Prime Minister Clark said the reports of Roy's charge were "absolutely incorrect." He added, "They certainly didn't make it to me because they knew I wouldn't have taken it seriously." Not that it would have mattered to the pragmatically oriented government; with Flora MacDonald still in Paris (where she'd been assured from Ottawa the previous day that everything was under control) the government would have fallen still — by one vote — even with the support of all five Socred members.

A week after the House was dissolved the Social Credit band was brutalized one more time by a public opinion poll showing their Quebec support had dropped from the 16 per cent of that province's vote they'd harvested in May to an abysmal 3.3 per cent.

After the government lost in the House, Clark supporters began a campaign for stable (read "majority") government. They tried to suggest that it had been the Clark government's minority status that had lead to its defeat. But six of Canada's last nine governments had been in a minority position. Only two of those had been defeated in the House: in 1974 Pierre Trudeau had carefully crafted the means of his own defeat, secure in the knowledge (correct as it developed) that he would be returned with a comfortable margin; in 1963, as in 1979, the government defeat came as a surprise — but not after Parliament had sat for only two months and four days, having failed to deal fully with a single piece of major legislation. And that's the rub in assessing the twenty-first government. Bills were introduced, speeches made, and debates held. But how does one measure the accomplishment of a Parliament that was destroyed before it had completed anything? It is like trying to get an insurance assessment for a piece of sculpture that has been shattered by an injudicious tap of the artist's chisel; would you insure the working drawings, knowing the sculptor might not be permitted by his peers to buy anymore marble?

The records of the intentions of the Clark government in Parliament were similar to those "working drawings." They were contained in the legislation introduced in the House by the government, in the statements made by ministers, even in the wide-eyed campaign material distributed after-the-fall by P.C. headquarters in Ottawa. There were, too, initiatives taken by the government both inside Parliament and out of it that bespoke both its priorities and its intentions.

For example, Joe Clark had promised more disclosure, more debate, more open government if elected. There were always nits to be picked but he was an ostentatious success as measured against any other Canadian government of the century. He had actually implemented some of that program and initiated moves to do more, before his defeat:

Item: Prime Minister Joe Clark was the first government leader in Canadian history to appear, voluntarily (or involuntarily, for that matter) before a parliamentary committee to answer questions about the budget and staff of the PMO. (Trudeau had always refused demands to do so.) The appearance came with some irony. The committee before which Clark testified was meeting in the former Liberal caucus room. The new P.M. was therefore seated with a huge, campaign photo blow-up of Pierre Trudeau — yellow rose in his lapel — smiling down over Clark's left shoulder; the walls around the rest of the West Block room were festooned with fusty portraits of Clark's Liberal predecessors in office. Grit members of the committee were not satisfied that the questioning had been sufficiently wide-ranging; but there had been questioning. A precedent had been set, and it would be harder for future P.M.s to duck disclosure. There'd been at least one surprise during the meeting. Joe Clark had told the committee his office staff comprised ninety-five people — up from the Trudeau staff of eighty-nine which High River Joe had attacked throughout the 1979 election campaign as an insulating shield of elitists around the then prime minister. Clark told the committee he'd played no numbers games in hiring staff: "Our strategy was present needs, not former numbers."

Item: Immigration Minister Ron Atkey resolved a nineteen-month-old dispute between the government and Human Rights Commissioner Gordon Fairweather in mid-September by agreeing to open his department's files so the commissioner could fully investigate complaints against immigration officials of discrimination. The Liberal government had launched a court battle to prevent the ex-Tory M.P. (whom they'd appointed to the post) from seeing the files. Gordon Fairweather told reporters there was "a whole new ball game in Ottawa now. I'm actually getting cooperation."

Item: Mr. Atkey ordered that the internal manuals outlining eligibility rules concerning both immigration and unemployment insurance be put into federal offices across Canada and made accessible to the public. In the past, applicants for immigrant status or unemployment insurance had fought their cases without knowledge of the standards and benchmarks being used by the civil servants who were controlling their lives. Investigative methods and screening techniques were deleted from the publicly displayed manuals, but Atkey ruled that anyone could demand up to ten photocopied pages of either manual free and get additional pages at cost.

Item: The government established a central registry of lobbyists in Ottawa; 1,500 had been registered by mid-November. In the past lobbyists had operated in the capital city under a variety of disguises dictated by the pious Canadian convention that there were no lobbies in Ottawa — a peculiar claim to anyone examining the city's phone book. It was not disclosed whether Executive Consultants Limited, of which PMO staff chief Bill Neville had been a founding partner, had registered. (Neville and his colleague Bill Lee had always claimed they did no lobbying; they simply offered advice to individual and corporate clients based on their experience as top flight executive assistants during the Pearson administration. But both were often observed to be uncommonly addicted to long and friendly telephone conversations with senior mandarins.)

Item: Despite its pious public posture, the government had at least one shot at restricting freedom of access to a parliamentary committee probe by using a piece of legislation its own Justice Minister had promised to scrap. Explanation: When Justice Minister Jacques Flynn was speaking on the government's Freedom of Information Act, which he introduced in the Senate October 24, he promised it would end the legal tradition of automatic Crown privilege — a means by which successive Canadian governments have been able to refuse to release documents or disclose information. "The government will not be able to hide behind absolute Crown privilege to withhold documents" anymore, said Senator Flynn. Meantime Parliament was moving to have prosecutions under Canada's mediaeval Official Secrets Act studied by a House of Commons committee. The committee chairman was Conservative M.P. Gerald Baldwin, Parliament's staunchest advocate of freedom of information and open government. Baldwin introduced a surprise motion in the House, getting unanimous approval, to establish the committee and to ensure that "no claims of Crown privilege [can] be allowed to limit the extent of the inquiry by the committee." A week later House Leader Baker told Baldwin the loophole-closing clause had to be dropped because "even a unanimous motion of the House cannot override Crown privilege, which is entrenched in law." The matter went into negotiation; it was still there when the government fell.

Item: In opposition, Sinclair Stevens had complained bitterly that Statistics Canada furnished unemployment data to the government a full day before it was released publicly or given to members of Parliament. In government, the Treasury Board boss, now in charge of Stats Canada, maintained the practice although he shortened the lead time some. It wasn't anymore a case of the government having "extra time to prepare excuses" for unpalatable figures. Now it was a case of the responsible ministers having "adequate notice to prepare responsible answers" for the opposition, once the numbers were made generally available.

As with other major legislation introduced by Joe Clark's government, the Freedom of Information bill died with the government. Although vastly more useful than the mostly cosmetic legislation under study by the Trudeau government, it was a considerably weakened instrument compared with its virile promise during the spring election campaign. It had too many loopholes by which cabinet ministers could refuse to release information. Instead of allowing petitioners to seek immediate remedy in the courts when refused information, it required them to appeal to a specially appointed commissioner who had powers only to recommend rather than to demand that government departments and agencies produce data. Only when those recommendations were refused would seekers-after-truth be allowed to try for a court order springing the documents they sought. But the bill went a long way toward permitting Canadians to require that documents assembled with their tax dollars, on their behalf, be made available to them. The legislation had passed through two readings in the House and would probably have gotten third reading and royal assent before Christmas had the government not been defeated. Sadly, seventy-nine-year-old Gerald Baldwin decided not to run in 1980 after having devoted much of his parliamentary career to pursuit of the legislation. But he vowed to stay in Ottawa and keep the next government of whatever stripe on notice that the Canadian public expected another — even better — bill when the House reconvened in March 1980.

Parliamentary reform had been another constant theme through Joe Clark's 1979 election campaign. Not many voters cared much about such rarified platform planks but Joe made good use of this one; the Trudeau government had been diminishing the House of Commons, said Clark, reducing it to a rubber stamp for decisions made by the non-elected elitists in the PMO. He, Joe Clark, would change that and "restore the supremacy of Parliament." He would allow, even encourage, Tory M.P.s to speak out when they disagreed with government policy. That might "cause us a little embarrassment" from time to time, but these men and women were, after all, "your M.P.s, not my M.P.s."

Former Diefenbaker cabinet sparkplug Alvin Hamilton, back in Parliament after a lengthy sabbatical as a newspaper columnist, tested that latter theory when he blasted the Clark government for its espousal of high interest rates. The high rates were a cause of very serious fractures within the Tory caucus. Attacked as iniquitous by Joe Clark in the previous Parliament and through the election campaign, they'd become an article of economic faith soon after the government took office. Prodded by Robert de Cotret and Bank of Canada Governor Gerald Bouey, Clark now bought the thesis that interest rates had to be kept higher in Canada than the United States to keep Canadian capital from bleeding away to New York in search of higher profits. If that happened, went the argument, the Canadian dollar would be forced even lower as against the U.S. dollar because of a worsening international balance of trade and payments; and a lower Canadian dollar would push inflation higher in a country where many of our consumer goods and much of our capital for economic and industrial expansion came from abroad.

Even if the whole argument was bought it was at best only tourniquet. The high interest rates might keep the dollar from falling further, but they did nothing to cure the basic malaise. The interest-rate policy was basically just a holding operation while waiting for things to get better, although it was presented by Finance Minister John Crosbie, when he was not under heavy and well-aimed pressure, as a kind of economic elixir.

But about Alvin Hamilton and the Tory fracture lines. Most western P.C.'s believed the interest rates were playing hell with the economy of the prairies. Many Ontario Tory M.P.s, denying the rates were stifling western development, bought the case they were needed and were anyway the lesser of evils. So Hamilton, never shy, agreed to play lightning rod for the western Tory dissidents and spoke out, publicly and strongly, against his government's policy. Joe Clark, who if he'd had a regional loyalty would have owed it to the west, told his weekly press conference that he wanted forthright comment like that from within his caucus. Clark scored high points for courage; but the private word was that Hamilton was sent to Coventry by his Tory colleagues that same day — and not without the knowledge of the leader.

The structural reforms of Parliament proposed by Joe Clark were described by the dean of House practices, New Democrat Stanley Knowles, as "superficial." Some of them were potentially valuable though, while others were variants on the classic good-news/bad-news jokes:

—Clark proposed that the House would be permitted to question cabinet ministers about their former portfolios, providing no one else could provide the information being sought. That was very good news. The Liberal government had avoided tough questioning over RCMP misconduct for years by playing musical solicitors general, so that former occupants of that Mountie-overseeing portfolio could refuse to answer questions as they were "not any longer the responsible minister." The new minister could meanwhile skate over the questions on the grounds he had not been the minister when the events in question took place. The bad news: Clark's new initiative would apply only to ministers still serving in the cabinet; immunity from questioning could still be arranged by having a minister revert to the status of an ordinary M.P.

—Speeches in the House would be shortened from a maximum of forty minutes to a maximum of twenty minutes in most cases. All good news.

—Question Period would be lengthened from forty-five minutes to sixty minutes daily. Okay, but already on slow days members were often developing intellectual hernias from the strain of trying to produce valid and interesting questions where none existed.

—Parliamentary committees would be restricted to maximum memberships of eleven (preventing much overlap and the spectacle of M.P.s missing two of three meetings at the same hour on the same day). The committees would also be given the right to initiate inquiries without needing Parliament's prior instruction or approval if fifty M.P.s (including ten or more from each of at least two parties) requested a probe. The bad news: the committees were refused the opportunity to hire permanent, expert staff, without which they'd never graduate to full effectiveness.

—The time allocated for the debate of private members' bills would be gathered into a full day's debate, once weekly, instead of the current one hour each day. The stated purpose was to make it possible that at least some private bills might thereby be passed instead of merely being talked out. With the one-hour rule, bills failing to reach a vote within the hour automatically dropped back to the bottom of the long list of those to be considered, effectively killing them. But under the proposed new system any party could still easily filibuster any private bill beyond the time now available to it. Still, the one-day-weekly debates would probably encourage opposition and backbench government members to work harder at the preparation of potential legislation and their speeches in its support.

It's academic, of course — all of it. The proposals for parliamentary reform died, too, with the government.

The one piece of legislation the Clark cabinet was determined to ramrod through Parliament was Bill C-20. This was the act to give Canadian home-owners tax credits in respect of the interest they paid on mortgages. Joe Clark had promised the measure in his election campaign — reportedly just forty-eight hours before the Liberals had planned a similar campaign pledge. Caught with a serious case of the campaign shorts, it's said, the Grits moved to oppose the plan instead. Given the way bank (and thereby mortgage) interest rates had been leapfrogging over the summer and autumn, it seemed the tax credits might barely cover the higher rates now being demanded from home-buyers. But the government believed the measure had won them urban seats in May. The government wasn't about to get found eating the scripts for anymore campaign promises in public places, either; so the bill had to be passed.

It almost was. Initially, the opposition stalled debate on

the bill. The government, anxious to get the tax-credit goodies into the income tax returns Canadians would be filing after the New Year, sent out forms taxpayers could use to claim the credits even though the measure wasn't yet law. If they waited for that, it would be too late to print and mail the forms in time for claims to accompany the April 1980 returns. The opposition was really mad, now; the government was defying Parliament and normal parliamentary practice, they said. The stall intensified.

Enough, said Clark. So the government announced it would apply closure. That is, it would introduce a motion to limit further debate on the bill, ending the filibuster. The opposition howled, but when the limiting motion was introduced the Social Credit joined the government M.P.s in supporting closure and the NDP and Liberals did not muster enough members to make the vote a contest. By a recorded vote of 120 to 85, on December 10, the House agreed that no more than one more day would be allowed for debate of Bill C-20.

Closure motions are not votes-of-confidence; but this one helped to trigger the real thing. "That night," said a research aide to an opposition party, "it was clear this government was going to roll right over anybody who got in their way. They really didn't think the opposition members were prepared to say 'shit' if they had a mouthful; they'd take anything that Clark and Baker pushed at them. A lot of M.P.s started getting blood in their eye that night. And it was just seventy-two hours later that they got their own back and defeated the government."

Now it would be up to that other kind of vote from the largest of all government constituencies — the country at large.

~ 9 ~

Clark and the Voters:
Victory by Default

The way to get things out of a government is to back
them to the wall, put your hands to their throats, and
you will get all they have.
        —Agnes MacPhail, speaking in Regina in 1927.

There are only two kinds of government — the scarcely
tolerable and the absolutely unbearable.
—John W. Dafoe, editor of the *Winnipeg Free Press*, circa 1940.

Evidence that Canadian voters had made a Dafoe choice
in May 1979 emerged with every addition to the polls flashing
past the prime ministerial limousine between May 22 and
December 13. Having exchanged the "absolutely unbearable"
Trudeau regime for the "scarcely tolerable" Clark succession,
the electorate seemed determined, after the event, to keep
the government's back to the wall, intimations of polling
booth strangulation dancing in PMO heads like visions of a

perverse Father Christmas.

Until fibre-glass optics and two-way data systems turn every living room in Canada into a computer link with instant analysis of how many T.V. viewers switch channels from the Prime Minister during Question Period, and how many from the leader of the opposition, we're left to the use of cruder devices to measure voter response between elections. There are the polls and, periodically, the by-elections (though these latter are really carnival mirrors of electoral reality, distorting hugely as voters decide, for example, that it's "safe" to admonish a government this time around as it can't be defeated — usually — by the loss of a single seat.)

Perusal of the opinion polls and surveys that bayed at the heels of the twenty-first government of Canada, seeming (to those besieged in the Langevin Block) like a pack of jackals feeding off the weak and feeble policies of the Clark government, makes it possible to construct one of those fever charts Sinc Stevens so loved to inflict on his cabinet colleagues. Starting with the Biggest Poll of All, the general election of May 22, the Tories progressed from "fair" condition to "serious," and then "critical" with a speed unrivalled in the history of Canadian government. Hindsight instructed that it had been in November, when the prognosis suddenly became desperate, that the patient had evidently lost the will to live.

In May the Clark Conservatives had won the election despite losing the battle of the polling booths. The Tories garnered 4 per cent fewer votes than the Liberals, but clustered their votes across a wider range of ridings so as to collect more seats in the final tallies. Thus the mandate Joe Clark so cheerfully acknowledged was no mandate at all, but merely the ricochet of a missile fired at Pierre Trudeau which fortuitously scattered the rose petals from the fallen leader's lapel into the eager hands of his rival. The score on May 22: Liberals — 40 per cent of the popular vote; Tories — 36 per cent.

What about the honeymoon factor? New governments

are usually given the benefit of the doubt, their first few months in office. The early spoils of victory include hugs, kisses, and general approbation. Voters don't like to feel dumb, so they are inclined to assume the government they've just elected must be pretty good. Just as with an expensive new car or a starchy new religion, new governments must be overpraised if anything, to justify the cost and the emotional commitment. All of which explains why just-elected political regimes generally enjoy a giddy high from the polls cast in their early months in office.

Well, in June, 1979, after just a couple of weeks in office, the Joe Clark government had soared all the way from 36 per cent of the popular vote (a month earlier) to a dizzying 38 per cent of public favour. The Liberals had held steady at 40 per cent and were never to look back in the next six months.

By July it seemed the honeymoon was over before the High River wrangler had even packed his bags for Lusaka and his fortnight as statesman. There had scarcely been time for a ritual kiss. The Tories were down three points in July, to 35 per cent; whereas the Liberals, coasting on a policy of resolute silence — they had been both invisible and mute since the election — were up to 43 per cent. Now there was an inconclusive, four-month saw-off. At October's end, things were within a pollster's range of-error of where they'd been when the returning officers limbered up their adding machines for election night. It was Conservatives 37 per cent; Grits 42 per cent.

In the meantime the Tories, taking note of a September survey which showed that half of all Canadians believed inflation was the key problem in our society (as compared with only 38 per cent, eight months earlier), hardened their resolve to bring down that no-nonsense budget they'd developed at Jasper in late August. The Prime Minister was also taking some internal heat by now over his continuing conviction that PetroCan must be sold. An early August opinion check across Canada had showed only 21 per cent of Canadians agreed with the policy while 48 per cent opposed the Clark plan. John Crosbie by now was telling reporters that the PetroCan sale was government policy, which he naturally supported; but he'd add with a smile, if pressed, that he wasn't *personally* persuaded the Crown corporation wasn't maybe doing a fairly good job and shouldn't be just left alone.

September showed, too, just how wrong Pierre Trudeau had been to peg his whole 1979 campaign on keeping-Canada-in-one-piece. Only one-quarter of Canadians believed national unity was the most serious problem facing the country. But curiously that total was up from a mere 17 per cent in May — this despite the government's absolute public refusal even to admit that the fuses for the Dominion's disintegration had been fabricated, let alone lit. That burrowing worry for Clark strategists aside, there was more good news for the hard-assed members of the cabinet who knew their tough economic siege was certain to fatten unemployment figures. Only 6 per cent of the nation's voters saw unemployment as the key concern in the country — a figure truly astonishing, given that on the same day 7 *per cent* of the labour force was out of work. But even to them the daily costs of consumer goods were a deeper preoccupation than the search for work.

While the pundits and opposition critics were hammering Joe Clark for his failure to meet Parliament sooner, the pollsters were building the case that he'd have been better not to call the House together at all. Because in the three weeks after the M.P.s assembled to hear the blanderized Throne Speech, Joe Clark's electoral fortune cookies crumbled into dust. In November the voters of Canada told those surveying them that now only 28 per cent of their number would cast Conservative ballots, down from 38 per cent just the month before. While the Tories were plumbing the depths of hope, searching the leaky pipe in efforts to plug the draining away of their futures, the Liberals had pumped up from 42 percentage points of popularity to 47 — more than enough, in Canada's history, to form a comfy majority government.

As November progressed the news got worse. Joe Clark, to his credit, beheaded no bearers of ill tidings, nor did he permit his discomfiture to cloud his predictions of economic and electoral nirvana just around the corner. On November 23 a new poll conducted by Goldfarb Associates was published in Toronto. Nothing in it was designed to comfort the PMO:

—Three in five people surveyed thought the new government had accomplished "very little." More depressing, among the affluent well-spring of Tory workers and donors, the disapproving total was 66 per cent.

—Although 68 per cent of the surveyed folk still wanted the tax credit on mortgage interest, which was Clark's policy centrepiece, more than half — a solid 53 per cent of all respondents — said they were disappointed: the plan now in the works fell short of the expectations for the policy raised by Clark's campaign promises, they said.

—Although Clark had already dropped the Israeli embassy move, a fat 71 per cent of those questioned wanted to register their disapproval anyhow.

—Almost as many, 68 per cent, were opposed to the government's intention to sell PetroCan.

Interestingly, the surveyors in their report noted the presence of "a significant minority, especially among young people, who are fed up with the government already. They wanted to see an election called right away to alter the government."

In December, before the House dissolved, a further study by the Gallup Poll showed the Tories had lost one more percentage point in public esteem. Now they were down to 27 per cent support in the days leading up to the Crosbie (de Cotret?) budget. They were well below the lowest level of approval accorded any Canadian government in the forty

© 1979. Reprinted with permission of the *Toronto Star* Syndicate.

years of poll-taking in the country.

The November poll figures had been explained away by the government as an aberration. When, in early January, the December numbers were made public, Joe Clark said they were also irrelevant as they'd been gathered before the budget and before the opposition's suicide pact in Parliament. But even by the weekend before Christmas, Joe Clark was again offering his refreshing and candid view that maybe some of it had to do with him. There was still an "image problem" the P.M. said:

> There clearly was a question as to just who I was when I ran for the leadership of the party. . . . It is an image rather than a substance problem. I've been able to deliver substantially in carrying out the work of leader of the party or as Prime Minister of the country, whether that work has been organizing and winning an election or organizing a government and in getting a program through.

The mind boggles! It was respectable for the victor of May 22 to claim he'd managed the task of "organizing and winning an election," even when it seemed from a less steamy observation post rather to have been lost by Pierre Trudeau and his Liberal sleep-walkers. But the notion of having "been able to deliver substantially in . . . organizing a government and getting a program through" was straight from Orwell's *1984* and the Orwellian invention of Newspeak. A government that had failed to pass legislation, failed to build alliances, and failed to deliver the legal base even for its most-cherished scheme (mortgage interest tax deductibility, now a dead letter vis-à-vis 1980 tax returns) was scarcely in a position to take credit for "getting a program through" Parliament. It was a pure case of Alice in Rideauland.

The Prime Minister barely had time to put his Christmas

stocking back into normal use before Carleton University's School of Journalism hit him with the heaviest load of all on Boxing Day 1979. The Carleton school had done a poll, too — and it had been conducted *after* introduction of the Crosbie budget speech and *after* the government had been defeated, the House dissolved, and the election called. Its results:

—The government party had only 22-per-cent support as against 38 points for the Liberals, 11 for the NDP, and 29 per cent undecided.

—Only a trifling 12 per cent thought Joe Clark was the best of the three leaders; he trailed New Democrat Ed Broadbent, who had 14 per cent of that contest, and was almost four hundred per cent behind Pierre Trudeau, at 44 per cent.

—Forty-four per cent of those asked said the government's performance had been "poor" and 39 per cent said "so-so." Just 11 per cent liked what the Clark administration had done.

All of the foregoing might be partially explained away by the peculiar nature of the capital city, where a heavy proportion of the population is made up of federal civil servants. The bureaucrats, remember, had knocked off a couple of Tory superstar candidates back in May 1979. But it was improbable that more than one-third of those polled worked in the public service and even those had likely cooled off from their earlier anxieties about Sinclair Stevens civil service cuts.

Even if the civil service bias of the capital could be used to explain away most of the Carleton survey data there was one result not amenable to that form of erasure. Civil servants, first, are generally conservative people who are supportive of "careful" policies; and Canadian civil servants, with incomes and pensions indexed to the cost of living, know themselves as well insulated as anyone against the hazards of inflation. So it was in Ottawa, if anywhere, that the Crosbie budget's hard-line should have been well received. However, a flat 50 per cent of respondents to the Carleton poll thought the Crosbie budget was "bad." Thirty-three per cent approved the Finance Minister's determination to control the federal deficit and boost energy prices. Seventeen per cent had no opinion.

In retrospect Joe Clark's screech-sodden junket to Newfoundland back in November must have seemed like a pleasure outing by contrast, despite the banquet at which one provincial Tory member fell loudly from the head table while Premier Peckford played the spoons on a wooden lectern inches from the Prime Minister's aching head.

Maybe no Canadian government had ever worried so much about the minutae of the voter response to its image while so thoroughly screwing up the larger issues — from the promised $2-billion tax-cuts-that-never-came to the aborted embassy move.

An example of loving devotion to the minute (Joe Clark's changing hair styles aside): In September and early October Clark's senior aides were terrified by the implied dangers of having three cabinet ministers in the Senate Chamber, 100 yards down the Centre Block corridor from the House of Commons, answering Liberal questions *there* while other Clark cabinet ministers might be giving different answers and interpretations *here* in the Commons. The press and public would die laughing — the government might just die. So aides in the PMO spent a considerable part of Indian summer investigating the practicality of taking a leaf from the pro football coaches and installing spotters in the galleries of both chambers. These observers, senior political aides all, watching the state-of-play in both houses, could be equipped with walkie-talkies through which they could signal dangerous fumbles from the Senate to the House and vice-versa. Advice on how best to punt out of the end zone could then be sent to the involved ministers in either House via the excellent system of page-persons. (There have been page-girls in the House now for several years.)

But while checking out the capacity of various makes and models of walkie-talkies — all good clean fun for the new boys on the bridge of our ship-of-state — the PMO permitted the P.M.'s promise to sell PetroCan to private interests to moulder over a period of six months.

Flogging the Crown corporation had been an old Clark fantasy. He'd first sternly urged the government to divest itself of the socialist viper at its breast his first year in Parliament back in 1972. During the 1979 election campaign, the Tory leader had never flagged in his energetic determination to sell the Crown corporation to private investors. Then, while the P.M. was at Lusaka in August, Energy Minister Ray Hnatyshyn told reporters that PetroCan wouldn't be broken up and sold, after all. Home from the conferences and fertility dances, Joe Clark said the government's policy was unchanged from whatever it had been before his departure — he didn't specify.

Now Sinclair Stevens joined battle. "I am supportive of Prime Minister Clark's position on PetroCan, which will be clarified in due course," said the Treasury Board chief who'd made "privatize" a household non-word. Asked to explain the policy, Stevens added only that: "Clark is always clear and I rest my case there."

It *was* a touch confusing. Initially, Joe Clark had simply wanted PetroCan scrapped, he said. Later he demanded that it be dismembered with the various bits-and-pieces sold to private enterprise. Then in late summer, the Prime Minister, determined above all to escape any taint of being indecisive, appointed a four-man task force to study how best to dispose of the government-owned Crown oil corporation. The task force eventually recommended that the P.M. give away shares in all PetroCan's profit-making operations to the public while setting up a new government agency to manage the functions that created losses.

Finally, the government defeated and with Christmas so close — and infinitely more engrossing than government policy — the P.M. was ready to have Michael Wilson produce a vastly transmogrified plan.

The final (?) Tory policy, announced after the election had been called, was a whole other proposal. If re-elected the government would give half PetroCan's shares to Canadians, sell one-fifth to anyone who wished to buy, and keep a controlling, 30 per cent interest in Ottawa. Nothing would really change except that the sale of shares would help PetroCan to raise money needed to expand the activities Joe Clark had earlier wanted stopped; and Canadians would spend about $125 million to distribute the "free" shares in a corporation they already had bought and funded through their taxes.

If the Jerusalem embassy move had become a metaphor for the Clark government's policy-making *apparat*, then PetroCan would likely stand as a monument to the Tory government's willingness to make what Ray Hnatyshyn had hailed as its "dramatic" new blueprint for energy self-sufficiency into a structure jerry-built to fit voter specifications.

Just as, pressured into a face-saving U-turn, Joe Clark had reversed his stance on Jerusalem: so with PetroCan. It had been the government's international constituency that had finally blocked the embassy move. It was the Canadian voters who had, through opinion surveys, letters-to-the-editor, and radio hotline shows, forced Clark to waffle, procrastinate, and finally devise a complex scheme to change things a lot without affecting them at all. *"La plus change . . ."*

The proximate cause of the death of the 1979 Clark government was the Crosbie budget and the opposition conviction that Canadian voters would not swallow high interest rates, high fuel prices, and gloomy forecasts. But there were those who suspected after surveying the cabinet-of-many-talents and all the failures of this most-promising Clark government, that the fault lay with the man himself.

~ 10 ~

The Coroner's Verdict

Canada's twenty-first government passed away shortly after nine o'clock on the evening of December 13, 1979. The post mortems had begun before the body was cool. An apparent victim of crib death, the toddler-Tory-administration was subject to all the clinical indignities of the autopsy room; no organic tissue was immune to the scalpel and probe, no nerve end left undisturbed. The coroner's verdict was confused. The agency-of-death was known; the blunt instrument of destruction had been identified — it was Her Majesty's Loyal Opposition. The lethal weapon had been examined, too; its structure and grain were under the microscope of public attention for weeks; its properties were understood as well as they probably ever could be. But who was the assailant? And what was the motive?

In time history will simplify the complexities. The management of minority government is one of the most delicate balancing acts in public life; and history would judge simply that Joe Clark had fallen off on a day when there was no Socred safety net. Whether the fall had been caused by faulty timing, miscalculation, a mis-step, the cruel gale of opposition, or the simple fact that the kid up there on the high wire just wasn't ready yet for the centre ring would be of little interest. The spotlight had been his, the fall his fall, the failure his to carry into history.

A respectable thesis, not mentioned in the reports of the coroner's jury, was simply that the kid hadn't cared enough — had been too detached up there — had been unable to link the intricate mechanics of his self-taught trade with a *feeling* for what was happening or what was coming next. There was a good knowledge of tradecraft — of how to place one's foot to accommodate the tension in the thin cable separating triumph from disaster; of how much resin was appropriate for certain levels of humidity — but little of the gut-sense and the conviction that separates the artist from the craftsman. There just wasn't enough juice flowing to create the sensitivity to nuance, to the invisible threat, that should have stretched every pore and raised every neck hair in preparation for crisis. The High River kid, up there, had never stopped giving an impression that maybe the whole thing had been a complex academic exercise, with even death an antiseptic climax to a nerveless, joyless exhibition.

One Clark-watcher put it much more succinctly: "He is a Gemini." And Geminis, it's clear, often suffer from terminal detachment; they are able to feel excitement but not passion; they are cut by the spurs of ambition but not healed by the joys of fulfilment or gratification.

Whatever the astrological portent of the stars ordering their heavenly protocol over High River on June 5, 1939, there *had* been a remote watchfulness about the 1979 Prime Minister. It had made Ontario's bumptious Tory caucus uncomfortable with him and kept a cadre of senior public service mandarins at arm's length — too far away to offer the transfusions of ideas and support he'd needed.

One observer said that Joe Clark's secret was that he had no secret. He was plainly ordinary. There was no riddle wrapped in the enigma; there was no layer of anything strange or even interesting under the veneer — just more veneer in one level after another all the way down to a central vacuum.

But that wasn't true. It wasn't just that Clark had come so far so fast to the biggest job in the country. He had skill and wit. There was a graceful ability to mock himself and a welterweight's fast footwork, a dancer's skill, on his good days in Parliament, that allowed him to jab and parry with the best the House had to offer. But the bobbing and weaving were self-taught, too. Clark wasn't "a natural." His half-grin, that unconscious signal to a debating opponent that he'd come up with the right turn-of-phrase, always telegraphed a punch; and when it spread to join the other side of his mouth, after the sally, the smile was that of a man who has just executed a perfect left hook. But not many in life had the dedication and discipline to achieve that state of skill; it wasn't to be scorned even if it fell short of the genius of inspiration.

But could a man whose first loyalty was to the manual of instruction care enough about the goals that his craft was meant to serve? Would he end, like that mythical engineer, up to his ass in alligators, by forgetting he was there to drain the swamp? It sometimes seemed so. Clark the tactician could coolly assess the best approach to the Quebec political maze. The technocrat in him could disavow a need to campaign to keep that province in Canada as "I am not resident in Quebec," but it couldn't explain to him the anger and incredulity that response evoked. Joe Clark gave evidence in his 1979 administration that he felt himself a stranger in the national family he now wanted to lead. There were none of the easy, subtle flashes of recognition from him to his Canadian relatives. He wanted the inheritance and the estate; and he would do his utmost to husband and administer it fairly for every other

THE PARTY'S OVER

member of the family; but there seemed to be, in the plainest language, *no love*. (Maybe Clark's refusal to swim in public was because of the tiny letters printed around his navel: "Made in Tory Backrooms, Inc.")

Joe Clark was between a rock and a hard place in his search for a leadership persona. On one side was John Diefenbaker the populist; the man who could never find a coatsleeve wide enough to display his heart, throbbing for the ordinary man, which he displayed every day of his political life with the same calculation given by other men to their choice of a tie. On the other was Pierre Trudeau, who casually carried his grace in some hidden pocket of his genes. But while Clark could wistfully envy Trudeau's innate style and then glory in having overcome the Bourbon with the unremitting, painful push-ups of the obsessive political fitness freak, he could also miss understanding Trudeau's central attraction. That was that people could forgive Trudeau his mischief, his crudeness, and even his arrogance because they believed he cared deeply for their mutual aspirations. Trudeau wore passion and dedication lightly, a bright rose in his psychic lapel; he was not embarrassed by it. Clark had endured self-doubt but never great pain or fear that anyone had recorded; like most men who'd lived their lives only in the centre of their emotional spectrum he mistrusted flamboyance. Although Trudeau had never been much further than a credit card's distance from succour, he had at least tested his will and body against northern rivers and desert heat; he'd learned that men may respectably weep and rage, and he'd been loved, by many, for that adult acceptance of his own humanity. (It had only been when, in 1978 and early 1979, voters began to believe he'd shed his nerve ends in the juiceless corridors of power that they had finally turned away from the hollow man who no longer had enough of his own substance left to echo their resonance.)

When the Clark government fell, the night of December 13, there'd been shock deep in the solemn eyes looking out through a face schooled to keep its own counsel; but no pain. Just shock. The next day, entering the final Tory caucus of the twenty-first government of Canada, he'd exhibited irritation (that substitute emotion of the a-involved man) and turned to a CBC T.V. camera just inches from his back. "Why don't you guys quit following me everywhere," he snarled. Then there was a half-second beat; the Prime Minister paused, adjusted his self-control, gave the intruding lens a meaningless smile which was followed by his back as he strode away to meet his fellow M.P.s.

At the end he resembled Ray Bolger in *The Wizard of Oz* — wanting to care, to love, to weep, but still searching for the sorcerer who would give him a heart implant. Many voters would have been more satisfied if *they* could like *him*, too. Admiration and respect were never quite enough.

Warner Troyer, one of Canada's leading and prolific journalists, has had his award-winning work appear in all media — television, radio, film, and print. He has contributed as reporter/director/writer/interviewer/ producer to such television programmes as *This Hour Has Seven Days, The Public Eye, W-5, The Fifth Estate,* and currently, *Point Blank.* He is author of two successful and acclaimed books, *No Safe Place* and *Divorced Kids.*